HOT ILLUSTRATIONS FOR YOUTH TALKS

WAYNE RICE

With contributions from Tony Campolo, Les Christie, Chap Clark, Jim Burns, Len Kageler, Ray Johnston, Rick Bundschuh, Dewey Bertolini and many more of America's top youth speakers!

Youth Specialties

El Cajon, California

Youth Specialties Books are published by Youth Specialties,
1224 Greenfield Drive, El Cajon, California 92021

Edited by Sharon Stultz, J. Cheri McLaughlin
Interior design and typography by Church Art Works
Cover design by Steve Hunt

Printed in the United States of America

ISBN: 0-310-40261-1

95 96 97 98 99 00 01 02/❖ DH / 12 11 10 9 8 7 6 5 4

YOUTH SPECIALTIES BOOKS

Professional Resources
Advanced Peer Counseling in Youth Groups
Called to Care
The Church and the American Teenager
(previously released as Growing Up in America)
Developing Spiritual Growth in Junior High
Students
Developing Student Leaders
Feeding Your Forgotten Soul
Help! I'm a Volunteer Youth Worker!
High School Ministry
How to Recruit and Train Volunteer Youth Workers
(previously released as Unsung Heroes)
Junior High Ministry (Revised Edition)
The Ministry of Nurture
Organizing Your Youth Ministry
Peer Counseling in Youth Groups
The Youth Minister's Survival Guide
Youth Ministry Nuts and Bolts
110 Tips, Time-savers, and Tricks of the Trade

Discussion Starter Resources
Amazing Tension Getters
Get 'Em Talking
High School TalkSheets
Junior High TalkSheets
More High School TalkSheets
More Junior High TalkSheets
Option Plays
Parent Ministry Talksheets
Tension Getters
Tension Getters Two
To Do or Not To Do

Special Needs and Issues
The Complete Student Missions Handbook
Divorce Recovery for Teenagers
Ideas for Social Action

Ideas Library
Ideas Combo 1-4, 5-8, 9-12, 13-16, 17-20, 21-24, 25-28,
29-32, 33-36, 37-40, 41-44, 45-48, 49-52
Ideas Index

Youth Ministry Programming
Adventure Games
Creative Bible Lessons
Creative Programming Ideas for Junior High
Ministry
Creative Socials and Special Events
Good Clean Fun
Good Clean Fun, Volume 2
Great Fundraising Ideas For Youth Groups
Great Games for City Kids
Great Ideas for Small Youth Groups
Greatest Skits on Earth
Greatest Skits on Earth, Volume 2
Holiday Ideas for Youth Groups (Revised Edition)
Hot Illustrations for Youth Talks
Hot Talks
Junior High Game Nights
More Junior High Game Nights
On-Site: 40 On-Location Youth Programs
Play It! Great Games for Groups
Play It Again! More Great Games For Groups
Road Trip
Rock Talk
Super Sketches for Youth Ministry

Teaching The Bible Creatively
Teaching the Truth about Sex
Up Close and Personal: How to Build Community
   in your Youth Group
The Youth Specialties Handbook for Great Camps &
   Retreats

4th - 6th Grade Ministry

Attention Grabbers for 4th - 6th Graders
4th - 6th Grade TalkSheets
Great Games for 4th - 6th Graders
How to Survive Middle School
Incredible Stories
More Attention Grabbers for 4th - 6th Graders
More Great Games for 4th - 6th Graders
More Quick and Easy Activities for 4th - 6th
Graders
Quick and Easy Activities for 4th - 6th Graders
Teach 'Toons

Clip Art

ArtSource Volume 1—Fantastic Activities
ArtSource Volume 2—Borders. Symbols, Holidays,
   and Attention Getters
ArtSource Volume 3—Sports
ArtSource Volume 4—Phrases and Verses
ArtSource Volume 5—Amazing Oddities and
   Appalling Images
ArtSource Volume 6— Spiritual Topics
Youth Specialties Clip Art Book
Youth Specialties Clip Art Book, Volume 2

Video

Edge TV Volumes 1-9
God Views
Next Time I Fall In Love Video Curriculum
Promo Spots for Junior High Game Nights
Resource Seminar Video Series
Understanding Your Teenager Video Curriculum
Witnesses

Student Books

Going The Distance
Good Advice
Grow for It Journal
Grow for It through the Scriptures
How to Live with Your Parents without
   Losing Your Mind
I Don't Remember Dropping the Skunk, But I
   Do Remember Trying to Breathe
Next Time I Fall in Love
Next Time I Fall in Love Journal
101 Things To Do During a Dull Sermon

CONTENTS

CONTRIBUTORS

Greg Miller
The Tractor Pull

Chuck Workman
The Battleship and the Lighthouse
Beware of Curare
Big Adventures
Hannibal's Fire

R. Davidson (Dave) Guild
Bought to Be Freed

Toby Wilson
Eskimo Wolf Hunters
When Do I Die?

Paul Warton
The Flying V
Sharpen Your Ax

Scott Hamilton
Coming Home

Skip Seibel
Not Much of a Man
Uncompromising Determination

Jeff Mugford
What Life?

Doug Roller
A Night in the Haunted House

Chap Clark
Brandon's Mess
Excuses, Excuses
Rudolph and Olive

Rick Bundschuh
The Big Rock
Deadly Marbles
France, 1943
The Lifeboat

Tony Campolo
The Circus Clown
The Oil Refinery
Teddy and Miss Thompson

Len Kageler
Computer Grace
The Grocery Store Clerk

Les Christie
Alexander the Great
The Bee Sting
The Blood of an Overcomer
The Boat in the Window
The Bottle
The Coffin
The Emperor Moth
Finish the Race
The Flying Wallendas
The Insurance Claim
The Jigsaw Puzzle
The Mirror
Out at Home Plate
The Painting of the Last Supper
Pepe Rodriguez
The Prince of Grenada
The Queen of England
The Society Woman
Telemachus Goes to Rome
Thermometers and Thermostats
Too Many Engineers

Mark Jevert
Awesome Obedience
The Blind Men and the Elephant
Face the Music
Getting the Word Out
The Job Applicant

Ray Johnston
An Answer to Prayer
Sparky, the Loser
We'll Get Back to You

Dewey Bertolini
Beauty and the Beast
Jesus and the Football Team

Jim Burns
Born to Fly
The Greatest Hitter in the World
The Painting of the Last Supper
The Suicide Attempt

Introduction

Nathan the prophet was the guest speaker. King David was the audience. Nathan had a message from the Lord to deliver to David, and, being the excellent communicator that he was, he opened with a story:

There were two men in a certain town, one rich and the other poor. The rich man had a very large number of sheep and cattle, but the poor man had nothing except one little ewe lamb he had bought. He raised it, and it grew up with him and his children. It shared his food, drank from his cup, and even slept in his arms. It was like a daughter to him.

Now a traveler came to the rich man, but the rich man refrained from taking one of his own sheep or cattle to prepare a meal for the traveler who had come to him. Instead, he took the ewe lamb that belonged to the poor man and prepared it for the one who had come to him (II Samuel 12:1-4).

The story, of course, had King David on the edge of his seat. He took it seriously and responded with gut-wrenching emotion: "As surely as the Lord lives, the rich scoundrel who took that little lamb deserves to die!" Bingo. The rest of Nathan's message required few words. All he had to do was apply the story to his audience: "You, sir, are that man."

Nathan knew what every good speaker and teacher knows: a picture is worth a thousand words. A captivating illustration that is thoughtfully chosen and skillfully used communicates more, is remembered longer, and has greater impact than thousands of words that may be truthful and important, but which are abstract and tell no story.

Jesus knew the value of a story, too. He spoke in parables. In fact, Matthew 13:34

records that Jesus never spoke without using a parable. He consistently sprinkled His talks with stories and illustrations to drive home the point He was making. He drew His illustrations from everyday life in the Middle East, describing farmers and families, sheep and goats, barns and wheat fields. People were amazed at His teaching.

Unfortunately, amazing is not often the word that teens use to describe speakers and teachers in the church today. The word "boring" seems to be more in fashion. A few popular speakers, however, know how to communicate well with kids, and invariably they use stories and illustrations effectively in their talks.

Hot Illustrations is a selection of stories that have been used effectively in youth talks by several of those popular speakers. I have used many of them myself. All of them can work with kids if the stories are chosen properly and communicated with conviction and purpose.

This is not an exhaustive collection of illustrations for youth talks. The books that claim to be exhaustive are often so large that they are difficult to use. One book on my shelf boasts nearly eight thousand illustrations in it. But to be honest, it's difficult to find one good illustration in that book when I need it. My goal for this book has been to offer you quality rather than quantity.

Selecting and using illustrations is a subjective and personal task; what works for you may not work for me (and vice versa). Even so, this book offers you a sampling of illustrations that I recommend without reservation. Much of that has to do with the quality of people who contributed to this book (their names are listed on pages 7 and 8). Good illustrations are extremely valuable and hard to come by. Many speakers prefer keeping them to themselves. That's why I'm grateful for these contributors who were willing to share some of their best illustrations with us.

How to Choose and Use Illustrations

AIM TO HIT YOUR TARGET

The most important thing to remember as you use the illustrations in this book is that they are only illustrations. They are not the points to be made. In other words, don't build your talk around these or any other illustrations. Begin with the point (the truth) that you want to communicate, and then find or create the illustration that supports that point.

A young boy received a bow and arrow from his father and immediately went outside to shoot it. A few minutes later, his father went outside and saw that the boy had shot his arrows at several targets that had been drawn on the side of a fence. To his amazement, each arrow had hit a bull's-eye. The father was impressed and said to his son, "I didn't realize you were such a good shot!" The boy replied, "Oh, it was easy. I shot the arrows first; then drew the targets around them."

When you use illustrations simply because they are good illustrations, you are drawing targets around your arrows. Begin planning a talk by deciding what the point (the target) is. Enhance the talk with an illustration only if it effectively drives home that point. Keep in mind that it takes different kinds of arrows to hit different kinds of targets. In the same way, be selective in filling your quiver with illustrations.

With each illustration in this book, I have suggested one or two points that can be supported by the illustration. Every illustration has multiple applications. A list of general topics that will help you to select illustrations more easily can be found on page 234.

DON'T OVER-ILLUSTRATE

Some points are so obvious that they don't need to be illustrated at all.

The truth of the above sentence may not be obvious, so I will illustrate. Suppose I stood up in front of a group and said, "God is good." The truth of that statement may not be clear to some people, so I would illustrate it with a story, example, or analogy that makes a picture in the listeners' minds that describes exactly what I mean when I say "God is good." On the other hand, if the temperature in the room is forty degrees, and I say to the group, "This room is cold," then I probably don't need to illustrate the truth of that statement with a story about someone freezing to death. My audience is not stupid; they know what I mean. The statement is self-evident. To illustrate would belabor the point.

Along with using illustrations only when necessary, use illustrations sparingly. One good illustration per point is plenty. People remember one illustration and may think about it for quite some time. You may remember, for instance, the one joke your friend told you over lunch—you may even tell it yourself to a few other friends. If your friend tells you two jokes, however, by the time you're done laughing at the second joke, you will have in all likelihood already forgotten the first one.

Remembering illustrations works the same way. If you use two or more illustrations, one right after another in the same talk, your audience is likely to forget them quickly. I recently listened to a speaker use twenty or more illustrations in one evening. Although he was entertaining, afterward I couldn't remember any of his illustrations. More significantly, I couldn't remember the point of any of them.

Choose your illustrations wisely. Make your point and illustrate it well, then move on to another point—or just stop. Don't pile illustration on illustration for the same point. Illustration-using is like driving a nail with a hammer—once the nail is in all the way, you stop pounding on it or you'll leave hammer marks in the wood. Some speakers leave hammer marks on their audiences by over-illustrating their points.

DON'T OVER-APPLY YOUR ILLUSTRATION

Audiences feel insulted when a speaker does all their thinking for them. You may assist your audience to get your point by proclaiming it as clearly as possible—like Nathan the prophet did. On the other hand, had Nathan not applied the illustration when he did, it is likely that David, after thinking about the story for a while, would have figured it out on his own. Nathan's illustration even speaks to us today when we don't limit its application to only King David's sin.

Jesus often told parables and stories without applying them at all. He allowed His audience to think about it for a while and discuss it among themselves. Jesus' own disciples were no doubt stimulated to learn by having to ponder the meaning of the parables. Of course, we are also the beneficiaries of this strategy of the Master Teacher.

USE ILLUSTRATIONS STRATEGICALLY

The primary reason for using an illustration is to drive home a point, but illustrations can be used for other purposes as well. You may use an illustration strictly for the purpose of holding a group's attention, for example, or for the purpose of providing a change of pace in your talk to make it more interesting.

I'm always amazed to watch how an audience that is dozing off, doodling on pieces of paper, or whispering to each other suddenly becomes alert when the speaker starts telling a story. As if on cue, all heads are raised and every eye is on the speaker. Things quiet down, and the speaker has everyone's undivided attention. Unfortunately, when the story ends, everyone goes back to what he or she was doing. A good speaker avoids this by making his or her application as poignant (without using the word "poignant") and interesting as the story itself. A properly chosen illustration causes the audience to "stay tuned" to discover what the point is.

Illustrations can also be used to set up a point the speaker is about to make. In other words, the illustration may not communicate much truth on its own, but because it's interesting or funny and serves as an icebreaker, it helps the speaker to segue into the point that she or he desires to make. Jokes, of course, are useful for that purpose. I have used "The Blind Date" illustration (page 38) many times to set up a talk on self-image or dating. Essentially a joke, it shouldn't be taken seriously on its own. Like any other illustration, you need to tie it in to your main purpose. The illustration should do some meaningful work.

Although illustrations may be used to hold a group's attention or to get laughs, if those are the only reasons they are used, the audience becomes frustrated and bored. Like the boy who cried "Wolf!" when there was no wolf, audiences eventually tire of speakers who have no content to their messages.

At a recent function I heard a well-known Christian author who is popular on the banquet circuit use dozens of jokes, stories, and illustrations. Although some of the illustrations were entertaining, his talk was disjointed and never went anywhere. He never had a point to make—or if he did, he never developed it so that the audience could remember what it was. He spoke for over an hour, and even though the speaker was extremely funny at times, I could tell that the audience had had enough. They wanted to go home. I concluded that this speaker was basically an insecure person whose primary concern was not to communicate a message, but to make the audience like him. He spent all his time trying to be entertaining rather than helpful. That's okay for a professional comedian, but not for someone who wants to be taken seriously.

CHOOSE THE RIGHT ILLUSTRATION

It goes without saying that you shouldn't use an illustration that is not right for you or your audience. Some of the illustrations in this book need to be communicated with a dramatic flair or with a sense of humor, for instance. If you have a difficult time being dramatic or funny, then you may want to avoid those illustrations. As you consider an illustration, ask yourself, *How comfortable will I feel using this one? Is this me?*

I remember trying to do Bill Cosby impressions when I was younger. I basically made a fool of myself. Why could Bill Cosby be so funny while I was bombing with the same routines? Because I'm not Bill Cosby. I can't be anyone else but me. When I speak to kids, I limit the illustrations I use to those that I feel comfortable with—those I can communicate with credibility and conviction. You may find that some illustrations in this book are difficult for you to communicate in that way. Stay away from them.

On the other hand, there are plenty of good illustrations you can use effectively. Once you select an illustration, rehearse it until you are comfortable with it and can present it convincingly. Memorize it if necessary. There's nothing worse than giving an illustration that makes no sense because you've left out a key element. I know; I've committed that error on more than one occasion. I've launched into an illustration only to discover that I had forgotten the part that made the illustration work. It's hard to go back and salvage the point.

Some of the illustrations in this book are meant to be read to the audience, such as "The Insurance Claim" on page 120. If you wish, photocopy the illustration and take it with you rather than read directly from the book.

CONSIDER YOUR AUDIENCE

Not all illustrations are appropriate for every audience. Although the illustrations in this book were selected because they are, generally speaking, effective with adolescents, that doesn't mean they deal with only adolescent concerns; it means that adolescents understand them and get the point if you communicate the story well.

Most of the illustrations in this book are stories, because adolescents love stories—particularly those with a lesson to teach. Teens enjoy making the connection between a concrete illustration and an abstract idea. For many youths, making that mental leap is a new and exciting experience, which makes storytelling an excellent way to teach this age-group.

Little children love stories too, but they haven't yet developed the intellectual ability to understand metaphorical or symbolic language. It's hard for them to figure out the meaning of an allegory or parable.

I once used "The Glove" (page 103) in a children's sermon. I demonstrated how a glove is useless until I put my hand in it. "In the same way," I explained to the children, "I can do nothing without Christ. I am like a glove, and Jesus is like the hand. With Christ in me, I can do anything that He wants me to do!" After the service I asked several of the children what they learned from my little talk. "A glove won't work," volunteered one little boy, "unless you put your hand in it." Oh well. The teens and the adults, however, commented on what a tremendous children's sermon it was. At least they got the point.

PERSONALIZE YOUR ILLUSTRATIONS

Illustrations are sometimes more effective if you personalize them. If you are telling "The Flying Wallendas" (page 96), you might say, "When I was a kid, I loved going to the circus when it came to town. I especially enjoyed watching the acrobatic teams who risked their lives every day flying on the high trapeze or walking the tightrope. What amazed me was that many of them performed their stunts without a safety net! One of the most famous of these acts was the Flying Wallendas." You can personalize a story that way without telling a lie.

An inappropriate personalization of a story might start like this: "I was there in Cobo Hall the night that the Flying Wallendas . . ."—unless, of course, you actually were there. Don't lie to make yourself look important, look good, or even look bad. Be honest with your audience, and you'll not only be more effective, but you'll have nothing that can come back later to haunt you.

A famous Christian youth speaker recently lost his entire ministry because it was discovered that much of what he had claimed to be true over the years was actually false. Illustrations are not important enough for you to lie for. Limit yourself to telling the truth. Anything short of that is unethical and has no place in the ministry of the church.

On the other hand, most illustrations aren't entirely true to begin with—even those that happened to you. None of the illustrations in this book are absolutely true. Some of them are based on historical events and on the lives of real people in history (such as "Alexander the Great" and "Telemachus Goes to Rome"), but they are presented here as illustrations, not history. They have undoubtedly been altered and embellished in order to make them effective illustrations. At best, they are only partially true. Tony Campolo likes to wink and say about his illustrations, "Well, if it didn't happen that way, it should have."

Few of the illustrations in this book actually happened. They are simply stories or parables that communicate truth. There's a difference between a true story and a story that communicates truth. It surprises some people that many of the stories Jesus told were not true. They were parables, and parables by definition are fictional. Jesus made those stories up. There never was an actual prodigal son, at least as far as we know. Jesus made up the story to illustrate a point and did it so well that it has become one of the most beloved stories of all time.

While we're dealing with personalizing illustrations, I will address the question of stealing someone else's illustration and using it as if it happened to you, or as if you thought of it. Is that wrong? Is that a form of plagiarism? I believe that the answer is yes—sometimes. I know several speakers who can hardly use their own talks anymore because people have "stolen" their illustrations and examples and made them their own. Tony Campolo laughs about the time he was about to deliver his famous "It's Friday, but Sunday's Comin,' " message to a church and was stopped by the pastor because the pastor said, "My congregation thinks that story happened to me."

The best way to use an illustration associated with someone else is to credit the source. If the above pastor had only said, "Tony Campolo tells a wonderful story about the time he . . ." Of course, that disclaimer might make the illustration less effective than it would have been if it was one's own, in which case it might be a good idea to avoid using it at all. This book contains few personal illustrations from individual speakers, unless they are relatively easy to transfer to another speaker. It's difficult to tell someone else's experience in the third person. These are illustrations that anyone can use. Don't worry about crediting the source, unless you feel that it's important to do so.

Another way to personalize an illustration is to think of a similar illustration from your own life. For example, "The Hopeless Baseball Game" on page 116 can become any baseball game you want it to be. Or it can become a golf game, a hockey game, or a Nintendo game. It doesn't really matter. If you can make the same point with a more personal illustration, do it.

You can also personalize illustrations by adding color to them, changing the details, renaming the characters, and generally making them more interesting to your audience. This is almost always a good idea when you tell a story from the Bible. Kids listen better when they can relate the story to people, places, and events they are familiar with. Teenagers easily identify with the prodigal son if they can imagine him as a high school student who has decided to drop out of school and leave home with his pockets full of cash.

Let the illustrations in this book encourage you to be on the lookout for illustrations that you can draw from your own life experiences and from the life experiences of others. Powerful illustrations can be derived from everyday life or from television, movies, books, magazines, or newspapers. Keep your eyes and ears open, and file away your discoveries for future use.

YOUR GOAL: COMMUNICATE THE TRUTH

Perhaps you have seen the "Far Side" cartoon by Gary Larson that depicts a dog sitting next to her owner with the caption "What we say to dogs." The owner is reprimanding the dog for her bad behavior with phrases like, "Bad dog, Ginger! I've had it with you! From now on you stay out of the garbage, or I'll take you to the dog pound! Do you understand me, Ginger? Do you?" The next panel shows the same scene with the caption "What dogs hear." In this version the owner's words are written out to show us what the dog is actually hearing: "Blah blah blah, Ginger! Blah blah blah blah blah, blah blah blah, Ginger, blah blah?"

Sometimes that's what happens when adults speak to kids. We need to keep in mind that our goal is to communicate the truth in such a way that what we say matches up accurately with what our students hear, understand, and apply. We hope that this book will help you to achieve that goal next time you stand in front of an adolescent audience.

Alexander the Great

Alexander the Great, one of the greatest military generals who ever lived, conquered almost the entire known world with his vast army. One night during a campaign, he couldn't sleep and left his tent to walk around the campgrounds.

As he was walking he came across a soldier asleep on guard duty—a serious offense. The penalty for falling asleep on guard duty was, in some cases, instant death; the commanding officer sometimes poured kerosene on the sleeping soldier and lit it.

The soldier began to wake up as Alexander the Great approached him. Recognizing who was standing in front of him, the young man feared for his life.

"Do you know what the penalty is for falling asleep on guard duty?" Alexander the Great asked the soldier.

"Yes, sir," the soldier responded in a quivering voice.

"Soldier, what's your name?" demanded Alexander the Great.

"Alexander, sir."

Alexander the Great repeated the question: "What is your name?"

"My name is Alexander, sir," the soldier repeated.

A third time and more loudly Alexander the Great asked, "What is your name?"

A third time the soldier meekly said, "My name is Alexander, sir."

Alexander the Great then looked the young soldier straight in the eye. "Soldier," he said with intensity, "either change your name or change your conduct."

☑ Application:

We who carry the name of Christ and call ourselves Christian must live up to the name. (See II Timothy 2:19; James 2:7; I Peter 4:16.)

An Answer to Prayer

A group of California high school students had spent three months preparing and planning to go to Mexico during Easter break to help the poor. They had prayed that God would use them in a mighty way. Anticipating an exciting week of ministry, they journeyed to a small church near Mexicali.

Upon arriving at the small rural village on a Sunday morning, the students saw that the church where they were going to serve had been badly burned. The roof had caved in, and only the four walls remained. They cautiously made their way into what was left of the building, while a hymn was being sung in Spanish. They were greeted by the puzzled stares of a weary, discouraged Mexican pastor and nine parishioners who were midway through their Sunday morning service. It was apparent that the congregation had never received the group's letters explaining their plans to serve and had no idea that the group was coming to spend the week with them.

At the end of the hymn, the pastor stopped the service, walked back to the group of high school students and said, "Qué pasa?" (which the group interpreted to mean, "What in the world are you rich white kids doing in our church?").

After a long silence, one of the students spoke: "We are Christians, and we are here to serve."

On hearing this the pastor's eyes brimmed with tears. "Some people in the village burned down our church six months ago," he explained. "We've been praying that God would send help, but we had given up hope that help was ever coming. Praise be to God!"

The thirty-five high school students were stunned silent. They had heard many times that God wanted to use them; now they were experiencing it for the first time. Amazed, one of the students turned to another and said, "I can't believe it. We're an answer to prayer!"

☑ Application:

God does want to use us, and He will—if we will only obey Him and follow Christ's example to be a servant. (See Philippians 2:3-11.) We can be the answer to someone's prayer by moving out of our comfort zones to use the gifts God has given us to make a difference in the world.

Awesome Obedience

A few centuries before Christ, Alexander the Great conquered almost all of the known world with his military strength, cleverness, and diplomacy. One day Alexander and a small company of soldiers approached a strongly defended, walled city. Alexander, standing outside the walls, raised his voice, demanding to see the king. The king, approaching the battlements above the invading army, agreed to hear Alexander's demands.

"Surrender to me immediately," commanded Alexander.

The king laughed. "Why should I surrender to you?" he called down. "We have you far outnumbered. You are no threat to us!"

Alexander was ready to answer the challenge. "Allow me to demon-strate why you should surrender," he replied. Alexander ordered his men to line up single file and start marching. He marched them straight toward a sheer cliff that dropped hundreds of feet to rocks below.

The king and his soldiers watched in shocked disbelief as, one by one, Alexander's soldiers marched without hesitation right off the cliff to their deaths. After ten soldiers had died, Alexander ordered the rest of his men to stop and to return to his side.

The king and his soldiers surrendered on the spot to Alexander the Great.

✓ Application:

The king and his soldiers realized that nothing would stop the eventual victory of men actually willing to give their lives for their leader.

Are you as dedicated to obeying Christ's commands as Alexander's soldiers were to obeying Alexander? Are you willing to be that committed to Christ? Think how much influence Christians could have in the world if they took seriously the commands of Jesus. "Be careful to obey . . . , so that it may always go well with you and your children after you, because you will be doing what is good and right in the eyes of the Lord your God" (Deut. 12:28).

The Battleship and the Lighthouse

In the darkest part of the night, a ship's captain cautiously piloted his warship through the fog-shrouded waters. With straining eyes he scanned the hazy darkness, searching for dangers lurking just out of sight. His worst fears were realized when he saw a bright light straight ahead. It appeared to be a vessel on a collision course with his ship.

To avert disaster he quickly radioed the oncoming vessel. "This is Captain Jeremiah Smith," his voiced crackled over the radio. "Please alter your course ten degrees south! Over."

To the captain's amazement, the foggy image did not move. Instead, he heard back on the radio, "Captain Smith. This is Private Thomas Johnson. Please alter your course ten degrees north! Over."

Appalled at the audacity of the message, the captain shouted back over the radio, "Private Johnson, this is Captain Smith, and I order you to immediately alter your course ten degrees south! Over."

A second time the oncoming light did not budge. "With all due respect, Captain Smith," came the private's voice again, "I order you to alter your course immediately ten degrees north! Over."

Angered and frustrated that this impudent sailor would endanger the lives of his men and crew, the captain growled back over the radio, "Private Johnson. I can have you court-martialed for this! For the last time, I command you on the authority of the United States government to alter your course ten degrees to the south! I am a battleship!"

The private's final transmission was chilling: "Captain Smith, sir. Once again with all due respect, I command you to alter your course ten degrees to the north! I am a lighthouse!"

☑ Application:

Many of us in today's world have little respect for authority. We operate as if rules can be (or should be) changed to fit our personal needs and desires. Commercials egg us on: "Have it your way." In reality, we can't always have it our way. We have to conform our lives to a higher truth, a higher authority—the Word of God.

God's truth is like a lighthouse. It's not going to change to accommodate us. We are the ones who must change to conform our lives to what God wants for us.

Jesus is also like a lighthouse. The Bible teaches that "Jesus Christ is the same yesterday and today and forever" (Heb. 13:8). He will always be there for us. He is absolutely dependable. We Christians must conform our lives to His will for us. If He tells us to alter our courses, we have no choice but to obey. That's what being a disciple is all about.

The Bear in the Cave

Two adventurous teenage boys who were good friends were out spelunking (exploring caves) when they found what appeared to be huge bear tracks deep inside a long, cavernous tunnel. They bravely decided to keep going, but they moved ahead slowly and with extreme caution, keeping their eyes and ears open in case they actually encountered a bear.

Suddenly, from the darkness behind a rock jumped the biggest, meanest-looking grizzly bear they had ever seen. Standing squarely in front of them, the bear beat on his chest and roared like a lion, sending a terrible sound echoing off the walls of the cave. Scared to death, the two boys decided they had better run for their lives. They immediately turned to make a dash for daylight.

Just then, one of the boys dropped to the floor and started untying his hiking boots. He whipped the boots off, jammed on his running shoes, and began tying the laces.

His exasperated friend yelled at him, "Come on, man! Let's get out of here! Why in the world are you changing shoes? We don't have much of a chance of outrunning that bear anyway!"

Lunging to his feet and starting to run, the first boy replied, "I don't have to outrun the bear. All I have to do is outrun you."

☑ Application:

Do you ever feel like your friends treat you like bear bait? When the going gets rough, they bail out on you. They remain friends with you until it costs them something—then they ditch you.

One of the great things about having Christ as your friend is knowing that He will never leave you nor forsake you (see Matt. 28:20 and Heb. 13:5). He is the friend who is not only willing to lay down His life for you, but He has done exactly that. "Greater love has no one than this, that he lay down his life for his friends" (John 15:13).

Beauty and the Beast

Do you remember the gripping scene in the animated Disney film *Beauty and the Beast* when the Beast was about to confess his love to Belle? Cogsworth looked on with euphoric anticipation, for if Belle pledged her love to the Beast, presto! The spell that hung over the castle like a dark, dank cloud of doom would finally be broken.

As she clasped hands with the Beast, Belle asked permission to gaze into the magical mirror in order to see her father. Viewing her father in obvious distress, she dropped the mirror and gasped at his plight. "I've got to go to him," she sobbed.

"Go to him, then," the Beast responded. Those four words spoke volumes.

Cogsworth later walked into the room with an air of triumphant expectancy as he declared to the Beast, "I must say that things are going swimmingly."

All hope vanished into thin air, however, when the Beast uttered the most significant line in the film. "I let her go," he confessed to his enchanted little clock.

As the reality of those words sunk in, Cogsworth shook himself and asked, "You did what?"

Can you imagine the impact of the Beast's admission? To let her go was to plunge his kingdom into another season of a cursed existence. To let her go meant that all hope was lost of ever becoming normally human again. To let her go meant that he forfeited his last, best chance of ever being loved. But he let her go. Why?

"I had to," he said. "I love her." The Beast understood that a lover does not hold the object of his love hostage to his possessive grasp.

☑ Application:

Perhaps a similar scene played itself out in heaven when God let go the beautiful angel Lucifer, who rebelled against God, determined to go his own way. "You did what?" Michael or Gabriel or some other angel might have asked, realizing that this action would bring untold misery and suffering upon God's creation.

What about you and me? Though God could force us to love Him, He lets us go. "I love them too much," He says. God loves us and allows us to go our own way, knowing full well that misery and suffering could be the result. Like Beauty, however, we have the option to come back, to change misery and suffering into joy and celebration. Whenever one person comes back to our loving heavenly Father, the angels rejoice (see Luke 15:10).

The Bee Sting

A vacationing family drives along in their car, windows rolled down, enjoying the warm breeze of the sunny day. All of a sudden, a big black bee darts in the window and starts buzzing around inside the car. A little girl, highly allergic to bee stings, cringes in the backseat. If she is stung, she could die within an hour.

"Oh, Daddy," she squeals in terror. "It's a bee! It's going to sting me!" The father pulls the car over to a stop, and reaches back to try to catch the bee. Buzzing around toward him, the bee bumps against the front windshield where the father traps it in his fist.

Holding it in his closed hand, the father waits for the inevitable sting.

The bee stings the father's hand and in pain, the father lets go of the bee. The bee is loose in the car again. The little girl again panics, "Daddy, it's going to sting me!" The father gently says, "No honey, he's not going to sting you now. Look at my hand."

The bee's stinger is there in his hand.

☑ Application:

Paul exulted in I Corinthians 15:55, "Where, O death, is your victory? Where, O death, is your sting?" Jesus says to us, "Look at my hands." He has Satan's sting, the sting of death, the sting of sin, the sting of deceit, the sting of feeling worthless. Jesus has all of those stingers in His hands. When you see that nail-scarred hand, realize that, on your behalf, Jesus took all the pain that Satan could throw at Him. He reduced Satan to a big black bee that's lost its stinger—all Satan can do is buzz. That's the victory that Jesus won for you.

Beware of Curare

In 1799 the famous Prussian explorer and scientist Baron Von Humboldt discovered a potent drug called curare.

On an expedition into the jungles of Venezuela, he watched an Indian hunter bring down a large animal with a single shot from his bow and arrow. The arrow had been poisoned with curare, a potion with two curious properties, derived from the jungle plants.

Curare injected into the bloodstream, as it was when hunting animals, was deadly. It immobilized the body, attacked the vital organs, and caused death almost instantaneously.

Humboldt discovered the second property of curare in a more dramatic fashion. He became sick, and a native witch doctor forced Humboldt to drink some curare that had been diluted with water. Terrified that he was going to die, Humboldt was surprised to find that after drinking the curare, he felt significantly better. Curare, when it was diluted and taken orally, he discovered, could have a positive medicinal value without causing any damage to vital organs.

The key to curare's impact lies principally in the way it is taken into the human body. Injected into the bloodstream, it's a deadly killer. Ingested orally, it's a soothing muscle relaxant.

☑ Application:

Christianity is a lot like curare. Its impact depends chiefly on how it is received. Many people choose to take it orally, diluted as much as possible, so that it has few side effects and makes them feel better—but that's not the purpose of true Christianity.

Christianity's purpose is to change us into new creations in Christ. In order for us to become new creations, we must die to our old selves and be born again, trading in our old lives for new ones. Those who want a "safe" Christianity that costs them little have a difficult time accepting death and new birth. True Christianity is not safe—it costs you your life. It cost God His only beloved Son, and it will cost you everything to follow Him. Paul wrote, "I have been crucified with Christ and I no longer live, but Christ lives in me" (Gal. 2:20a).

Don't settle for a watered-down version of Christianity. It can't be taken orally. It has to be injected.

Big Adventures

Outside magazine often features stories about people who risk their lives in order to establish a reputation for themselves.

Larry Walters, for instance, took flight in a lawn chair suspended by forty-two large helium-filled balloons. Upon reaching an altitude of 16,000 feet, he began popping the balloons with a pellet gun, descending to the ground safely.

Frenchman Jean Luc Antoni skis down rocks. In 1987 he set a world record of sixty-one miles per hour riding a mono-ski down a rocky slope in France. Because braking is impossible, the resourceful Antoni erected a cardboard retaining wall at the bottom of the run and smashed into it. He survived.

Reg Mellor, age seventy-two, is the reigning world champion of "ferret legging." Ferret legging is a contest involving "the tying of a competitor's trousers at the ankles and the subsequent insertion into those trousers of a couple of particularly vicious, fur-coated, foot-long carnivores called ferrets. The brave contestant's belt is then pulled tight, and he proceeds to stand in front of the judges as long as he can, while these animals with claws like hypodermic needles and teeth like number sixteen carpet tacks try to get out."

Reg Mellor holds the world record at five hours, twenty-six minutes.

☑ Application:

Activities like these seem crazy, but lots of kids today, in their quest for adventure, engage in crazy behaviors—abusing drugs and alcohol, for instance—that make ferret legging seem sane by comparison. Reg Mellor's legs are permanently scarred by years of ferret legging, but his scars are mild compared to the internal scars left on kids who use drugs.

If you have ever seen an addict going through drug withdrawal, you have seen the ferrets tearing at his insides. If you have ever seen someone whose brain has been "fried" on drugs, then you have seen someone whose brain has been attacked by ferrets.

Don't get me wrong, though. Risk and adventure comprise an important element of life. In fact, people who follow Jesus Christ undertake the greatest and riskiest adventure of all.

The Big Rock

A little boy was spending his Saturday morning playing in his sandbox. He had with him his box of cars and trucks, his plastic pail, and a shiny, red plastic shovel.

In the process of creating roads and tunnels in the soft sand, he discovered a large rock in the middle of the sandbox. The lad dug around the rock, managing to dislodge it from the dirt. With no little bit of struggle, he pushed and nudged the rock across the sandbox by using his feet. (He was a very small boy and the rock was very large.) When the boy got the rock to the edge of the sandbox, however, he found that he couldn't roll it up and over the little wall.

Determined, the little boy shoved, pushed, and pried, but every time he thought he had made some progress, the rock tipped and then fell back into the sandbox. The little boy grunted, struggled, pushed, shoved—but his only reward was to have the rock roll back, smashing his chubby fingers. Finally he burst into tears of frustration.

All this time the boy's father watched from the living room window as the drama unfolded. At the moment the tears fell, a large shadow fell across the boy and the sandbox. It was the boy's father. Gently but firmly he said, "Son, why didn't you use all the strength that you had available?"

Defeated, the boy sobbed back, "But I did, Daddy, I did! I used all the strength that I had!"

"No, son," corrected the father kindly. "You didn't use all the strength you had. You didn't ask me."

With that the father reached down, picked up the rock, and removed it from the sandbox.

✔ Application:

Do you have "rocks" in your life that need to be removed? Are you discovering that you don't have what it takes to lift them? God is always available to us and willing to give us the strength we need to overcome obstacles and to accomplish great things for Him. "God is our refuge and strength, an ever-present help in trouble" (Psalm 46:1).

The Blind Date

(A joke for guys to tell—in the first person, as if it happened to you.)

Since I was a little shy when I was in high school, I didn't ask many girls out on dates. So my friend came up to me one day and said, "Hey, I've lined you up with a great date for Saturday night. It's all set."

"Who is it?" I asked. It turned out to be his cousin Doris. I had never met her. In fact, I had never met any girl named Doris. "Oh, no," I said, "I'm not going on a blind date."

"Hey, don't worry about this one," my friend said. "Doris is a terrific girl. And trust me—she's a real looker. But if you don't believe me, I'll tell you how to get out of the date if you don't like the way she looks. This is what I do: I go to a girl's front door to pick her up, and when she opens the door, I check her out. If I like what I see, then great, we're all set. But if she's ugly, I fake an asthma attack. I go 'Aaahhhhggggggg!' (Hold your throat like you're having trouble breathing.) The girl asks, 'What's wrong?' And I say, 'It's my asthma.' And so we have to call off the date. Just like that. No problem."

"Well, I don't know . . . but okay, it sounds easy enough. I'll do it," I said.

So I went to pick up Doris. I knocked on the door, and she came to the front door. I took a look at her, and to my surprise, my friend was right. She was beautiful! I stood there not knowing exactly what to say.

She took one look at me and went, "Aaahhhhggggggg!"

✔ Application:

Chances are you've also been rejected by other kids because you weren't good looking enough, or athletic enough, rich enough, or "cool" enough—whatever that is.

God doesn't look at us that way, though. When He takes a look at us, He thinks we're beautiful. He accepts us the way we are. God isn't concerned with how we look on the outside. He's much more concerned about what's inside: "Man looks at the outward appearance, but the Lord looks at the heart" (I Sam. 16:7b). God wants us to have a heart like His—one that reaches out and loves all people, regardless of their looks.

The Blind Men and the Elephant

In an ancient village, a parable tells, all the people were blind. One day while walking on the road, six men from that village came upon a man riding an elephant. The six men, who had heard about elephants but had never been close to one, asked the rider to allow them to touch the great beast. They wanted to go back to their village to tell the other villagers what an elephant looked like.

The rider agreed and led each of the six men to a different part of the elephant. All the blind men touched and stroked the elephant until they were certain they knew what the animal looked like.

In great anticipation they returned to their village to report their experience. The villagers gathered around to hear about the elephant. The first man, who had felt the animal's side, said, "An elephant is like a great thick wall."

"Nonsense," said the second man, who had felt the elephant's tusk. "He is rather short, round, and smooth, but very sharp. I would compare an elephant not with a wall but with a spear!"

The third man, who had touched the ear, took exception. "It is nothing at all like a wall or a spear," he said. "It is like a gigantic leaf made of thick wool carpet. It moves when you touch it."

"I disagree," said the fourth man, who had handled the trunk. "I can tell you that an elephant is like a giant snake."

The fifth man shouted his disapproval. He had touched one of the elephant's legs and concluded, "An elephant is round and thick, like a tree."

The sixth man had been allowed to ride on the elephant's back, and he protested, "Can none of you accurately describe an elephant? Clearly he is like a gigantic moving mountain!"

To this day, the men continue to argue, and no one in the village has any idea what an elephant looks like.

☑ Application:

The Bible describes God in many different ways—because He is experienced in many different ways. He is the Creator of the universe, but He is also the faithful friend. He is the righteous judge, but He is also the forgiving Father. For us to understand God, or for us to understand the Bible, we must carefully study the Word of God in its entirety. Whenever we perceive only one view of God, or one view of the truth, we are likely to be misled.

One of the reasons that so many people still don't understand the Gospel is because Christians can't agree on what it is. We Christians must strive to find the common ground between us and to present a united front to the world. Jesus prayed that all of us may be one: "May they be brought to complete unity to let the world know that you sent me and have loved them even as you have loved me" (John 17:23b).

The Blood of an Overcomer

Louis Pasteur's coworker in the demonstration of what used to be called the germ theory was Dr. Felix Ruh, a Jewish doctor in Paris. The physician's granddaughter had died of black diphtheria, and Dr. Ruh, vowing he would find out what had killed his granddaughter, locked himself in his laboratory for days. He emerged with a fierce determination to prove, with his colleague Louis Pasteur, that the germ theory was more than a theory.

The medical association had disapproved of Pasteur and had succeeded in getting him exiled, but he did not go far from Paris. He hid in the forest and erected a laboratory in which to continue his forbidden research.

Twenty beautiful horses were led out into the forest to the improvised laboratory. Scientists, doctors, and nurses came to watch the experiment. Ruh opened a steel vault and took out a large pail filled with black diphtheria germs, which he had cultured carefully for months. There were enough germs in that pail to kill everyone in France. The scientist went to each horse and swabbed its nostrils, tongue, throat, and eyes with the deadly germs. Every horse except one developed a terrific fever and died. Most of the doctors and scientists wearied of the experiment and did not remain for what they thought would be the death of the remaining horse.

For several more days this final horse lingered, lying pathetically on the ground. While Ruh, Pasteur, and several others were sleeping on cots in the stables, the orderly on duty had been instructed to awaken the scientists should there be any change in the animal's temperature during the night.

About two A.M. the temperature showed a half degree decrease, and the orderly awakened Dr. Ruh. By morning the thermometer had dropped two more degrees. By night the fever was entirely gone, and the horse was able to stand, eat, and drink.

Then Dr. Ruh took a sledgehammer and struck that beautiful horse a deathblow between the eyes. The scientist drew all the blood from the veins of this animal that had developed the black diphtheria but had overcome it. The scientists drove as fast as they could to the municipal hospital in Paris. They forced their way past the superintendent and the guards and went into the ward where three hundred babies lay, segregated to die from black diphtheria. With the blood of the horse, they forcibly inoculated every one of the babies. All but three lived and recovered completely.

They were saved by the blood of an overcomer.

☑ Application:

We have been saved by the blood of an overcomer. Jesus Christ overcame sin and death on the Cross, and by His blood we are saved. (See Ephesians 1:7.)

The Boat in the Window

A young boy spent many hours building a little sailboat, crafting it down to the finest detail. He then took it to a nearby river to sail it. When he put it in the water, however, it moved away from him very quickly. Though he chased it along the bank, he couldn't keep up with it. The strong wind and current carried the boat away. The heartbroken boy knew how hard he would have to work to build another sailboat.

Farther down the river, a man found the little boat, took it to town, and sold it to a shopkeeper. Later that day, as the boy was walking through town, he noticed the boat in a store window.

Entering the store, he told the owner that the boat belonged to him. It

had his own little marks on it, but he couldn't prove to the shopkeeper that the boat was his. The man told him the only way he could get the boat was to buy it. The boy wanted it back so badly that he did exactly that.

As he took the boat from the hand of the shopkeeper, he looked at it and said, "Little boat, you're twice mine. I made you and I bought you."

☑ Application:

In the same way, we are twice God's. Our Father in heaven both created us and paid a great price for us. (See Colossians 1:16 and Romans 5:8.) With the blood of His Son, we have been redeemed and reunited with God.

Jesus Christ gave His life to get us back, yet so often we show such little gratitude for what He has done for us.

Bonny's Bunny

A friend of mine was sitting in the living room one day when his cat dragged in a little "gift" in its mouth—a dead animal of some sort. Taking a closer look, he was dismayed to recognize the dead animal to be a bunny that belonged to a little girl who lived next door. Her name was Bonny. My friend felt terrible, believing his cat had killed little Bonny's bunny.

My quick-thinking friend came up with a plan. Removing from the cat's mouth the dead animal, which by now was a dirty mess, he put it in the kitchen sink. With a little warm water and some shampoo, he tried to clean up the dead bunny as best he could. Then he took a hair dryer (a "hare dryer" actually) and blow-dried the bunny until it looked pretty good. Finally, he took the dead bunny out to the neighbor's rabbit hutch and placed it back in the cage. He kind of fluffed him up so that he looked very natural there in his little box.

The next morning, my friend looked out the window and noticed a crowd of people gathered around the rabbit hutch. Everyone seemed to be talking and pointing. My friend decided to go over and act like any normal curious neighbor and find out what was going on.

When he got there, Bonny's mother said to my friend, "You won't believe what has happened! It's a miracle! Bonny's bunny passed away a few days ago, and we buried that little bunny right over there . . . "

✔ Application:

Have you ever tried to cover up one sin with another? Covering up only makes matters worse. When we get caught doing something wrong, for example, we may attempt to cover it up with a lie. But just like Bonny's bunny, the result is never what we expected. We end up looking foolish. We would have been better off admitting we were wrong and accepting the consequences.

Born to Fly

One day a prairie chicken found an egg and sat on it until it hatched. Unbeknownst to the prairie chicken, the egg was an eagle egg, abandoned for some reason. That's how an eagle came to be born into a family of prairie chickens.

While the eagle is the greatest of all birds, soaring above the heights with grace and ease, the prairie chicken doesn't even know how to fly. In fact, prairie chickens are so lowly that they eat garbage.

Predictably, the little eagle, being raised in a family of prairie chickens, thought he was a prairie chicken. He walked around, ate garbage, and clucked like a prairie chicken.

One day he looked up to see a majestic bald eagle soar through the air, dipping and turning. When he asked his family what it was, they responded, "It's an eagle. But you could never be like that because you are just a prairie chicken." Then they returned to pecking the garbage.

The eagle spent his whole life looking up at eagles, longing to join them among the clouds. It never once occurred to him to lift his wings and try to fly. The eagle died thinking he was just a prairie chicken.

☑ Application:

You were born to fly. But some of you think and act like prairie chickens because the world keeps telling you that's what you are. God created you "a little lower than the angels" (see Psalm 8 and Hebrews 2:7). Do you ever feel like there's something more to life than what you are experiencing? Look up! Lift your wings and fly! God wants you to be all that you were created to be.

The apostle Peter writes in I Peter 1:14, "As obedient children, do not conform to the evil desires you had when you lived in ignorance." In other words, "Stop living like eagles who think they are prairie chickens." You are no longer ignorant. You know who and what you are. You are born again through the living and enduring Word of God. Now live that way. Spread your wings and fly.

The Bottle

A small bottle containing urine sat upon the desk of Sir William Osler, the eminent professor of medicine at Oxford University. Sitting before him was a class full of young, wide-eyed medical students, listening to his lecture on the importance of observing details. To emphasize his point, he announced: "This bottle contains a sample for analysis. It's often possible by tasting it to determine the disease from which the patient suffers."

He then dipped a finger into the fluid and brought it into his mouth. He continued speaking: "Now I am going to pass the bottle around. Each of you please do exactly as I did. Perhaps we can learn the importance of this technique and diagnose the case."

The bottle made its way from row to row, each student gingerly poking his finger in and bravely sampling the contents with a frown. Dr. Osler then retrieved the bottle and startled his students by saying, "Gentlemen, now you will understand what I mean when I speak about details. Had you been observant, you would have seen that I put my index finger in the bottle but my middle finger into my mouth!"

☑ Application:

Many people live their lives just like the students in Professor Osler's class. They think they have life all figured out, but they have forgotten one important detail: the need to allow Christ to change them into the kind of people that God wants them to be. As a result, life is toxic and bitter.

God doesn't hide the way from us, however, or try to deceive us as Professor Osler did his students. The Bible clearly gives us instructions for living a life with purpose and meaning. All we need to do is to open our eyes, to think, and to pay attention to what God has to say to us. "Taste and see that the Lord is good!" (Ps. 34:8).

Bought to be Freed

Back in the 1800s, a young Englishman traveled to California in search of gold. After several months of prospecting, he struck it rich. On his way home, he stopped in New Orleans.

Not long into his visit, he came upon a crowd of people all looking in the same direction. Approaching the crowd, he recognized that they had gathered for a slave auction. Slavery had been outlawed in England for years, so this young man's curiosity drew him to watch as a person became someone else's property. He heard "Sold!" just as he joined the crowd. A middle-aged black man was taken away.

Next a beautiful young black girl was pushed up onto the platform and made to walk around so everyone could see her. The miner heard vile jokes and comments that spoke of evil intentions from those around him. Men were laughing as their eyes remained fixed on this new item for sale.

The bidding began.

Within a minute, the bids surpassed what most slave owners would pay for a black girl. As the bidding continued higher and higher, it was apparent that two men wanted her. In between their bids, they laughed about what they were going to do with her, and how the other one would miss out. The miner stood silent as anger welled up inside of him. Finally, one man bid a price that was beyond the reach of the other. The girl looked down. The auctioneer called out, "Going once! Going twice!"

Just before the final call, the miner yelled out a price that was exactly twice the previous bid. An amount that exceeded the worth of any man. The crowd laughed, thinking that the miner was only joking, wishing that he could have the girl himself. The auctioneer motioned to the miner to come and show his money. The miner opened up the bag of gold he had brought for the trip. The auctioneer shook his head in disbelief as he waved the girl over to him.

The girl walked down the steps of the platform until she was eye-to-eye with the miner. She spat straight in his face and said through clenched teeth,

"I hate you!" The miner, without a word, wiped his face, paid the auctioneer, took the girl by the hand, and walked away from the still-laughing crowd.

He seemed to be looking for something in particular as they walked up one street and down another. Finally he stopped in front of some sort of store, though the slave girl did not know what type of store it was. She waited outside as the dirty-faced miner went inside and started talking to an elderly man. She couldn't make out what they were talking about. At one point the voices got louder, and she overheard the store clerk say, "But it's the law! It's the law!" Peering in, she saw the miner pull out his bag of gold and pour what was left of it on the table.

With what seemed like a look of disgust, the clerk picked up the gold and went in a back room. He came out with a piece of paper, and both he and the miner signed it.

The young girl looked away as the miner came out the door. Stretching out his hand, he said to the girl, "Here are your manumission papers. You are free." The girl did not look up.

He tried again. "Here. These are papers that say you are free. Take them."

"I hate you!" the girl said, refusing to look up. "Why do you make fun of me!"

"No, listen," he pleaded. "These are your freedom papers. You are a free person."

The girl looked at the papers, then looked at him, and looked at the papers once again. "You just bought me . . . and now, you're setting me free?"

"That's why I bought you. I bought you to set you free."

The beautiful young girl fell to her knees in front of the miner, tears streaming down her face. "You bought me to set me free! You bought me to set me free!" she said over and over.

The miner said nothing.

Clutching his muddy boots, the girl looked up at the miner and said, "All I want to do is to serve you—because you bought me to set me free!"

☑ Application:

At one time we were all slaves to sin and to death. But Christ came to redeem us—to pay for our freedom. He bought us with His own blood, that we might be free. "For you know that it was not with perishable things such as silver or gold that you were redeemed . . . but with the precious blood of Christ, a lamb without blemish or defect" (I Pet. 1:18, 19).

The Boy and the Circus

A little boy who lived far out in the country in the late 1800s had reached the age of twelve and had never in all his life seen a circus. You can imagine his excitement, when one day a poster went up at school announcing that on the next Saturday a traveling circus was coming to the nearby town. He ran home with the glad news and the question, "Daddy, can I go?" Although the family was poor, the father sensed how important this was to the lad. "If you do your Saturday chores ahead of time," he said, "I'll see to it that you have the money to go."

Come Saturday morning, the chores were done and the little boy stood by the breakfast table, dressed in his Sunday best. His father reached down into the pocket of his overalls and pulled out a dollar bill—the most money the little boy had possessed at one time in all his life. The father cautioned him to be careful and then sent him on his way to town.

The boy was so excited, his feet hardly seemed to touch the ground all the way. As he neared the outskirts of the village, he noticed people lining the streets, and he worked his way through the crowd until he could see what was happening. Lo and behold, it was the approaching spectacle of a circus parade!

The parade was the grandest thing this lad had ever seen. Caged animals snarled as they passed, bands beat their rhythms and sounded shining horns, midgets performed acrobatics while flags and ribbons swirled overhead. Finally, after everything had passed where he was standing, the traditional circus clown, with floppy shoes, baggy pants, and a brightly painted face, brought up the rear. As the clown passed by, the little boy reached into his pocket and took out that precious dollar bill. Handing the money to the clown, the boy turned around and went home.

What had happened? The boy thought he had seen the circus when he had only seen the parade!

✔ Application:

Are you experiencing all that God has for you? The Christian life is a marvelous adventure, an exciting journey. Many people—including Christians—seem to be content to float in a sea of mediocrity, settling for second best. Do you want the abundant life that Jesus promised? Do you want to live life to its fullest? Then aim higher. Don't set your sights too low. Determine to become all that God created you to be. Give yourself to Christ, follow Him completely, and allow the Holy Spirit to work in you and through you. You ain't seen nothin' yet!

Brandon's Mess

There was once a dad who had a three-year-old son named Brandon.

One day, Brandon sees his dad eating chocolate chip cookies in the living room and says to himself, *Daddy loves chocolate chip cookies with milk. So I'm going to give Daddy a glass of milk.* With that thought Brandon goes into the dining room and drags a chair from the dining room into the kitchen, leaving a trail of scratch marks on the floor.

Brandon climbs up on the chair and hitches himself onto the counter to pull at the cabinet door. Wham! It smashes against the adjacent cabinet door, leaving a gash where the handle hit it. Brandon reaches for a glass, accidentally knocking two others off the shelf. Crash! Tinkle, tinkle! But Brandon doesn't care. He's thinking, *I'm going to get Daddy some milk!*

Meanwhile, Brandon's dad is watching all this, wondering if he should step in and save the rest of his kitchen. He decides, for the moment, to watch a little more as Brandon scrambles off the chair, dodging the pieces of broken glass, and heads for the refrigerator.

Pulling violently on the refrigerator door, Brandon flings it wide open—and it stays open, of course. Brandon puts the glass on the floor—out of harm's way, supposedly—and grabs, not the little half gallon of milk, but the big gallon container that is full of milk. He rips open the top, pours it in the vicinity of the glass, and even manages to get some milk in the glass. The rest goes all over the floor.

Finally done, Brandon puts the milk carton on the floor and picks up the glass yelling, "Daddy, I got something for you!" He runs into the living room, trips, and spills milk all over the place—the floor, the sofa, his dad.

Brandon stands up and looks around. He sees broken glass, milk everywhere,

cabinets open, his dad with milk from his eyebrows to his toes, and starts to cry. Through his tears, he looks up at his dad with that pained expression that says, "What are you going to do to me?"

His dad only smiles. He doesn't see a kid that just destroyed his house. Instead he sees a beautiful little boy whom he loves very much. It doesn't matter what he's done. Brandon's dad stretches his arms out to hold his little boy tight and says, "This is my son!"

☑ Application:

When we talk about God as our Father, the kind of father we're talking about is Brandon's father. God is a father who loves us unconditionally, even though we make a real mess of things. Jesus told a similar story about another son who messed up. We call the story "The Prodigal Son." It also could be called "The Parable of the Loving Father" because, just like Brandon's dad, the father in the story threw his arms around his son and said, "This is my son!" (See Luke 15:11-32.)

Caught in a Blizzard

A man hiking out of the Chugach mountains of Alaska hoped to make it to camp before a deadly blizzard hit. He was too late. The blizzard struck with such a fury that he was unable to see even two feet in front of his face. The windblown snow and ice knocked him off his feet as he struggled to find his way. Although he knew that he was only a short distance from camp, he had lost his sense of direction and couldn't determine which way to go. Finally, in the dark of night, he slumped down into a snow bank—cold, wet, and totally exhausted. He could go on no further. He resigned himself to die.

As he lay there in the snow, he thought he heard something—a faint cry, like the whimpering of a puppy. He called out to it and tried to crawl toward the sound. Sure enough, it was a dog that was also lost in the storm. The puppy had somehow been separated from its mother and was freezing to death. The man quickly began rubbing the dog's fur, trying to keep the dog's blood circulating so that the dog would survive. He warmed the dog with his breath, continuing through the night to try to keep the little puppy alive.

The next day scouts from the village found both the man and the dog alive. They discovered that the man, by working to keep the little dog alive during the night, had kept himself alive as well.

☑ Application:

When we serve others, we do a lot of good for them. More importantly, perhaps, we ourselves are changed. We benefit. We grow. We become more like Christ. If you are feeling spiritually empty, you may need to stop thinking about yourself and serve others. The way to spiritual health is to give yourself away.

The Chicken and the Pig

A chicken and a pig were walking down the street one day and noticed some poor children who looked as if they hadn't eaten anything for days.

Moved with compassion, the chicken said to the pig, "I have an idea! Let's give those children a nice breakfast of ham and eggs."

The pig contemplated the chicken's suggestion and said, "Well, for you, that would involve a small sacrifice; but for me, it would involve total commitment!"

☑ Application:

When Jesus came to save us from sin, He knew that it would cost Him His life. He went to the cross anyway to offer to us eternal life. His commitment to us was total.

Like the pig in the story, our commitment to Christ must be more than a small sacrifice of our time, energy, and money. It must involve our whole life—all that we are. When we come to Christ, we must be willing to live out the same total commitment that Jesus modeled. Jesus said, "If anyone would come after me, he must deny himself and take up his cross and follow me" (Matt. 16:24).

Choosing Mary

The following letter appears in a book by Dan Taylor called Letters to My Children *(InterVarsity Press, 1989). Dan is writing to his son Matthew.*

Dear Matthew,

When I was in the sixth grade I was an all-American. I was smart, athletic, witty, handsome, and incredibly nice. Things went downhill fast in junior high, but for this one year at least, I had everything.

Unfortunately, I also had Miss Owens for an assistant teacher. She helped Mr. Jenkins, our regular teacher. She knew that even though I was smart and incredibly nice, there was still a thing or two I could work on.

One of the things you were expected to do in grade school was learn to dance. My parents may have had some reservations at first, but since this was square dancing, it was okay.

Every time we went to work on our dancing, we did this terrible thing. The boys would all line up at the door of our classroom. Then, one at a time, each boy would pick a girl to be his partner. The girls all sat at their desks. As they were chosen, they left their desks and joined the snot-nosed kids who had honored them with their favor.

Believe me, the boys did not like doing this—at least I didn't. But think about being one of those girls. Think about waiting to get picked. Think about seeing who was going to get picked before you. Think about worrying that you'd get picked by someone you couldn't stand. Think about worrying whether you were going to get picked at all!

Think if you were Mary. Mary sat near the front of the classroom on the right side. She wasn't pretty. She wasn't real smart. She wasn't witty. She was nice, but that wasn't enough in those days. And Mary certainly wasn't athletic. In fact, she'd had polio or something when she was younger; one of her arms was drawn up, and she had a bad leg, and to finish it off, she was kind of fat.

Here's where Miss Owens comes in. Miss Owens took me aside one day and said, "Dan, next time we have square dancing, I want you to choose Mary."

She may as well have told me to fly to Mars. It was an idea that was so new and inconceivable that I could barely hold it in my head. You mean pick someone other than the best, the most pretty, the most popular, when my turn came? That seemed like breaking a law of nature or something.

And then Miss Owens did a really rotten thing. She told me it was what a Christian should do. I knew immediately that I was doomed. I was doomed because I knew she was right. It was exactly the kind of thing Jesus would have done. I was surprised, in fact, that I hadn't seen it on a Sunday school flannel board yet: "Jesus choosing the lame girl for the Yeshiva dance." It was bound to be somewhere in the Bible.

I agonized. Choosing Mary would go against all the coolness I had accumulated.

The day came when we were to square dance again. If God really loved me, I thought, He will make me last. Then picking Mary will cause no stir. I will have done the right thing, and it won't have cost me anything.

You can guess where I was instead. For whatever reason, Mr. Jenkins made me first in line. There I was, my heart pounding—now I knew how some of the girls must have felt.

The faces of the girls were turned toward me, some smiling. I looked at Mary and saw that she was half-turned to the back of the room, her face staring down at her desk. Mr. Jenkins said, "Okay, Dan—choose your partner."

I remember feeling very far away. I heard my voice say, "I choose Mary."

Never has reluctant virtue been so rewarded. I still see her face undimmed in my memory. She lifted her head, and on her face, reddened with pleasure and surprise and embarrassment all at the same time, was the most genuine look of delight and even pride that I have ever seen, before or since. It was so pure that I had to look away because I knew I didn't deserve it.

Mary came and took my arm, as we had been instructed, and she walked beside me, bad leg and all, just like a princess.

Mary is my age now. I never saw her after that year. I don't know what her life's been like or what she's doing. But I'd like to think she has a fond memory of at least one day in sixth grade. I know I do.

Taken from *Letters to My Children* by Daniel Taylor. © 1989 by Daniel Taylor. Used by permission of InterVarsity Press, P.O. Box 1400, Downers Grove, IL 60515

☑ Application:

The good news of the Gospel is that we have been chosen by God. You are someone special in the eyes of God. God looked out over all the world and for some crazy reason saw you and me and said, "I choose Jennifer; I choose Nathan; I choose _____. " The greatest day of your life was the day when God chose you. Yes, you have the opportunity to choose to accept Christ as Savior, but you have that privilege because He has chosen you first. "You did not choose me, but I chose you and appointed you to go and bear fruit—fruit that will last" (John 15:16).

The Circus Clown

The philosopher Søren Kierkegaard once told a story about a circus that caught fire. The flames from the circus fire spread to the fields surrounding the circus grounds and began to burn toward the village below.

The circus master, convinced that the village would be destroyed and the people killed unless they were warned, asked if there was anybody who could go to the village and warn the people. The clown, dressed in full costume, jumped on a bicycle and sped down the hill to the village below.

"Run for your lives! Run for your lives! A fire is coming and the village is going to burn!" he shouted as he rode up and down the streets of the village. "The village is going to burn! Run for your lives!"

Curious villagers came out from their houses and shops and stood along the sidewalks. They shouted back to the clown, laughing and applauding his performance. The more desperately the clown shouted, the more the villagers cheered.

The village burned and the loss of life was great because no one took the clown seriously. After all, he was just a clown.

☑ Application:

Like the clown in the story, pastors and priests play a role in the church that negates their message when they go out into the world. We cannot expect the clergy, therefore, to tell the story of the Gospel to the world; the world doesn't take them seriously.

Instead, it's up to us—ordinary people—to take Jesus seriously and to go and preach the Gospel to the world. (See Mark 16:15.) We can't expect the world to take the Gospel seriously if we are unwilling to tell others about Christ and to be a witness to His power and love.

The Cliff

A man named Jack was walking along a steep cliff one day when he accidentally got too close to the edge and fell. On the way down he grabbed a branch, which temporarily stopped his fall. He looked down and to his horror saw that the canyon fell straight down for more than a thousand feet. He couldn't hang onto the branch forever, and there was no way for him to climb up the steep wall of the cliff.

So Jack began yelling for help, hoping that someone passing by would hear him and lower a rope or something. "HELP! HELP! Is anyone up there? HELP!" He yelled for hours, but no one heard him. He was about to give up when he heard a voice.

"Jack. Jack. Can you hear me?"

"Yes, yes! I can hear you. I'm down here!"

"I can see you, Jack. Are you all right?"

"Yes, but . . . who are you, and where are you?"

"I am the Lord, Jack. I'm everywhere."

"The Lord? You mean, GOD?"

"That's Me."

"God, please help me! I promise—if You'll get me down from here, I'll stop sinning. I'll be a really good person. I'll serve You for the rest of my life."

"Easy on the promises, Jack. Let's just get you down from there; then we can talk. Now, here's what I want you to do. Listen carefully."

"I'll do anything, Lord. Just tell me what to do."

"Okay. Let go of the branch."

"What?"

"I said, let go of the branch. Just trust Me. Let go."

There was a long silence. Finally Jack yelled, "HELP! HELP! IS ANYONE ELSE UP THERE???"

☑ Application:

Have you ever felt like Jack? We say that we want to know the will of God, but when we find out what it is, we can't handle it. It sounds too scary, too difficult. We decide to look elsewhere.

A good part of discipleship is simply trusting God—trusting that He knows what's best for us. Jesus says, "Take my yoke upon you and learn from me. . . . For my yoke is easy and my burden is light" (Matt. 11:29, 30). This simply means that God isn't trying to make life difficult or impossible for us. He will always be there for us. When He says, "Let go of the things that stand between you and Me, and trust Me with your life," it sounds pretty scary. But when we let go, we find freedom and safety in His hands.

The Coffin

One episode of the old "Alfred Hitchcock Presents" TV show was about a pretty woman serving a life sentence in prison. Angry and resentful about her situation, she had decided that she would rather die than to live another year in prison.

Over the years she had become good friends with one of the prison caretakers. His job, among others, was to bury those prisoners who died in a graveyard just outside the prison walls. When a prisoner died, the caretaker rang a bell, which was heard by everyone. The caretaker then got the body and put it in a casket. Next, he entered his office to fill out the death certificate before returning to the casket to nail the lid shut. Finally, he put the casket on a wagon to take it to the graveyard and bury it.

Knowing this routine, the woman devised an escape plan and shared it with the caretaker. The next time the bell rang, the woman would leave her cell and sneak into the dark room where the coffins were kept. She would slip into the coffin with the dead body while the caretaker was filling out the death certificate. When the caretaker returned, he would nail the lid shut and take the coffin outside the prison with the woman in the coffin along with the dead body. He would then bury the coffin. The woman knew that there would be enough air for her to breathe until later in the evening when the caretaker would return to the graveyard under the cover of darkness, dig up the coffin, open it, and set her free.

The caretaker was reluctant to go along with this plan, but since he and the woman had become good friends over the years, he agreed to do it.

The woman waited several weeks before someone in the prison died. She was asleep in her cell when she heard the death bell ring. She got up, picked the lock of her cell, and slowly walked down the hallway. She was nearly caught a couple of times. Her heart was beating fast. She opened the door to the darkened room where the coffins were kept. Quietly in the dark, she found the coffin that contained the dead body, carefully climbed into the coffin, and pulled the lid shut to wait for the caretaker to come and nail the lid shut.

Soon she heard footsteps and the pounding of the hammer and nails. Even though she was very uncomfortable in the coffin with the dead body, she knew that with each nail she was one step closer to freedom. The coffin was lifted onto the wagon and taken outside to the graveyard. She could feel the coffin being lowered into the ground. She didn't make a sound as the coffin hit the bottom of the grave with a thud. Finally she heard the dirt dropping onto the top of the wooden coffin, and she knew that it was only a matter of time until she would be free at last.

After several minutes of absolute silence, she began to laugh. She was free! She was free!

Feeling curious, she decided to light a match to find out the identity of the dead prisoner beside her. To her horror, she discovered that she was lying next to the dead caretaker.

The final scene faded to black as you heard the woman screaming.

☑ Application:

Typical of Hitchcock's horror stories, this one has an unexpected ending—an unhappy one.

Many people believe they have life all figured out. They plan to sin, to live their lives by their own rules, and by so doing gain freedom and happiness. In the end, however, they discover the grisly truth—sin only leads to death and destruction.

Through Christ we may escape from the penalty of sin. We can have freedom and happiness through Him: "If the Son sets you free, you will be free indeed" (John 8:36). Don't let sin take you to the grave. There is no escape once the dirt is tossed on top of the coffin. "For the wages of sin is death, but the gift of God is eternal life in Christ Jesus our Lord" (Rom. 6:23).

Coming Home

A story is told about a soldier who was finally coming home after having fought in Vietnam. He called his parents from San Francisco.

"Mom and Dad, I'm coming home, but I've a favor to ask. I have a friend I'd like to bring home with me."

"Sure," they replied. "We'd love to meet him."

"There's something you should know," the son continued. "He was hurt pretty badly in the fighting. He stepped on a land mine and lost an arm and a leg. He has nowhere else to go, and I want him to come live with us."

"I'm sorry to hear that, Son. Maybe we can help him find somewhere to live."

"No, Mom and Dad, I want him to live with us."

"Son," said the father, "you don't know what you're asking. Someone with such a handicap would be a terrible burden to us. We have our own lives to live, and we can't let something like this interfere with our lives. I think you should just come on home and forget about this guy. He'll find a way to live on his own."

At that point, the son hung up the phone. The parents heard nothing more from him. A few days later, however, they received a call from the San Francisco police. Their son died after falling from a building, they were told. The police believed it was suicide.

The grief-stricken parents flew to San Francisco and were taken to the city morgue to identify the body of their son. They recognized him, but to their horror they also discovered something they didn't know—their son had only one arm and one leg.

☑ Application:

The parents in this story are not unlike many of us. We find it easy to love those who are good-looking or fun to have around, but we don't like people who inconvenience us or make us feel uncomfortable. We would rather stay away from people who aren't as healthy, beautiful, or smart as we are.

Thankfully, God doesn't treat us that way. God loves us with an unconditional love that welcomes us into His forever family, regardless of how messed up we are.

Because of His great love for us, we are to reach out to others in the same way.

Computer Grace

Just about everyone enjoys playing computer games. One of the best is Microsoft's "Flight Simulator." In most versions of the game, you can choose a prop plane or a Lear jet, and you can also choose which of 180 airports around the country to take off from or to attempt a landing at.

Only after acquiring landing skills after many hours of practice can a player avoid crashing the plane and land safely. It's all very realistic. You can crash into the Empire State Building in New York City, the Sears Tower in Chicago, or the Space Needle in Seattle. Your plane can break apart in midair, breaking the sound barrier over Dallas. You can nose-dive into Lake Michigan going five hundred miles per hour.

The greatest thing about "Flight Simulator," though, is that the game always restores you. No matter what happens, you can start all over again. Whenever you crash and burn, fall apart, or splash into the ocean, the game always puts you back together and places you back on the runway ready to take off again.

☑ Application:

That's the way it is with the Lord. He's absolutely faithful to forgive us and to restore us when we mess up and to get us back into action, hopefully a little wiser after our failures and bad decisions. (See I John 1:9.) With Christ we are never out of the game. "And the God of all grace, who called you to his eternal glory in Christ, after you have suffered a little while, will himself restore you and make you strong, firm and steadfast" (I Pet. 5:10).

The Cookie Snatcher

While waiting at the airport terminal for her plane to begin boarding, a woman sat reading a newspaper. Earlier, she had purchased a package of cookies in the airport snack shop to eat after she got on the plane. Out of the corner of her eye, she noticed that the man sitting next to her was eating a cookie. She looked down and noticed that her package of cookies had been opened and the man was eating them.

The woman couldn't believe that the man would have such nerve as to eat her cookies. So that she wouldn't lose all of her cookies to the man, she slowly reached over, took a cookie, and ate one herself. To her amazement, the man continued to eat more cookies. Getting more and more irritated, the woman removed all but one cookie from the package and ate them.

At that point, the man reached down and took the last cookie. Before eating it, though, he broke it in half and left half of the cookie for the woman. This made the woman so angry, she grabbed the empty package with the half cookie and crammed it in her purse.

Then, to her shock, she noticed that there in her purse was her unopened package of cookies.

☑ Application:

Sometimes when we judge or condemn others, we end up judging or condemning ourselves. The Bible speaks of this in Luke 6:37: "Do not judge, and you will not be judged. Do not condemn, and you will not be condemned." Have you ever been too quick to pass judgment on another? When we do that, we put ourselves in a precarious and often embarrassing position. Check out all the facts, ask questions, listen carefully, and give people the benefit of the doubt.

Deadly Marbles

(This is based on a true story.)

The Mexican man who loaded the scrap metal from a southern Arizona junk pile into his beat-up pickup truck bed was excited. This big haul would mean food on the table and money in his pocket once he transferred the metal into cash at the scrap metal recycler in Mexico.

As the truck pulled onto the highway, little steel balls from an antique dental X-ray machine began to drop onto the ribbed bed of the truck. These tiny, radioactive marbles bounced among the shifting sheets of metal and rolled back and forth in the truck bed. Some of them spilled along the highway.

After the scrap metal had been transformed into pesos, the man hurried back to his village, metal balls still rolling in the grooves of the truck bed. In no time at all the children discovered the shiny, bright treasures—and the game of marbles became popular in the village. The balls were a coveted addition to any child's collection of glassies, cat's eyes, peewees, and jumbos.

Before long, many in the town began to complain of similar symptoms: red rash, fatigue, loss of hair, vomiting. After many months and several deaths in the village, the truth was discovered: dozens of people were suffering from severe radiation poisoning.

The pretty little balls, held, traded, and treasured, turned out to be both delightful and deadly.

☑ Application:

Sin is a lot like those little metal balls. Although it often appears to be harmless, innocent, and fun to play with, it's always a deadly poison (see Job 20:12-15).

The Diamond Merchant

A rich Dutch merchant was seeking to buy a diamond of a certain kind to add to his collection. A famous dealer in New York found such a stone and called him to come and see it.

The merchant flew immediately to New York, where the seller had assigned his best diamond expert to close the transaction. After hearing the assistant describe in perfect technical detail the diamond's worth and beauty, the Dutchman decided not to buy it. Before he left, however, the owner of the store stepped forward and asked, "Do you mind if I show you that stone once more?" The customer agreed.

The store owner didn't repeat one thing that the salesman had said. He simply took the stone in his hand, stared at it, and described the beauty of the stone in a way that revealed why this stone stood out from all the others he had seen in his life. The customer bought it immediately.

Tucking his new purchase into his breast pocket, the customer commented to the owner, "Sir, I wonder why you were able to sell me this stone when your salesman could not?"

The owner replied, "That salesman is the best in the business. He knows more about diamonds than anyone, including myself, and I pay him a large salary for his knowledge and expertise. But I would gladly pay him twice as much if I could put into him something I have which he lacks. You see, he knows diamonds, but I love them."

☑ Application:

When it comes to sharing Christ with others, the issue is not how much we know about Jesus, but how much we love Him. God is not interested in how much we know but in how much we love. When we truly love Jesus, we love others as well, and that is how the good news of the Gospel is spread. (See I John 4:7-12.)

The Emperor Moth

A man found a cocoon of an emperor moth and took it home so he could watch the moth come out of the cocoon. One day a small opening appeared. The man sat and watched the moth for several hours as it struggled to force its body through that little hole. Then it seemed to stop making any progress. To the man it appeared as if the moth had gotten as far as it could in breaking out of the cocoon and was stuck.

Out of kindness the man decided to help the moth. He took a pair of scissors and snipped off the remaining bit of the cocoon so that the moth could get out. Soon the moth emerged, but it had a swollen body and small shriveled wings. The man continued to watch the moth, expecting that in time the wings would enlarge and expand to be able to support the body, which would simultaneously contract to its proper size.

Neither happened. In fact, that little moth spent the rest of its life crawling around with a swollen body and shriveled wings. It was never able to fly.

The man in his kindness and haste didn't understand that the restricting cocoon and the struggle required for the moth to get through the tiny opening were God's way of forcing fluid from the body into the wings so that the moth would be ready for flight once it achieved its freedom from the cocoon.

☑ Application:

Just as the moth could only achieve freedom and flight as a result of struggling, we often need to struggle to become all God intends for us to be. Sometimes we wish that God would remove our struggles and take away all the obstacles; but just as the man crippled the emperor moth, so we would be crippled if God did that for us. God doesn't take away our problems and difficulties, but He promises to be with us in the midst of them and to use them to restore us, making us into better, stronger people (see I Peter 5:10).

Eskimo Wolf Hunters

According to tradition, this is how an Eskimo hunter kills a wolf.

First, the Eskimo coats his knife blade with animal blood and allows it to freeze. He then adds layer after layer of blood until the blade is completely concealed by the frozen blood.

Next, the hunter fixes his knife in the ground with the blade up. When a wolf follows his sensitive nose to the source of the scent and discovers the bait, he licks it, tasting the fresh frozen blood. He begins to lick faster, more and more vigorously, lapping the blade until the keen edge is bare. Feverishly now, harder and harder, the wolf licks the blade in the cold Arctic night. His craving for blood becomes so great that the wolf does not notice the razor-sharp sting of the naked blade on his own tongue. Nor does he recognize the instant when his insatiable thirst is being satisfied by his own warm blood. His carnivorous appetite continues to crave more until in the morning light, the wolf is found dead on the snow!

☑ Application:

Many kids begin using drugs, drinking alcohol, smoking cigarettes, or engaging in unsafe sexual behavior for the same reasons that the wolf begins licking the knife blade. It seems safe and delicious at first, but it doesn't satisfy. More and more is desired, leading to a crisis—or death.

Don't be fooled by the temptations of sin. Like the wolf, we can get away with it for a while. Eventually, however, its true character is revealed. Sin leads to death and destruction. "For the wages of sin is death" (Rom. 6:23).

Excuses, Excuses

The following is a collection of actual excuses for missing school that were turned in by students and reported in *Seventeen* magazine:

My son is under a doctor's care and could not take P.E. yesterday. Please execute him.

Please excuse Cynthia for being absent. She was sick and I had her shot.

Please excuse Tom for being absent on Jan. 28, 29, 30, 31, 32, and 33.

Please excuse Danny for being. It was his father's fault.

June could not come to school yesterday because she was bothered by very close veins.

Richard had an acre in his side.

Please excuse Timothy for being absent last week. He could not talk because of Larry and Gitus.

Please excuse Nancy for staying home. The doctor said that her lungs are too full to be outside.

Please excuse Margaret from Jim yesterday because she is administrating.

Please excuse Robert for being absent. He had a cold and could not breed well.

☑ Application:

People have all sorts of excuses for the things they do. Some are legitimate, some are not. A teenage boy in Washington was recently acquitted of murder charges on the grounds that he was "morally handicapped." It wasn't his fault—said the judge—that he shot and killed a fellow student. He had an excuse.

Life, perhaps unfortunately in some minds, doesn't work that way. Sooner or later we all have to take responsibility for who we are and what we do. We can't keep blaming our behavior on someone or something else.

Scripture teaches that we will be held accountable to God for our actions. (See Romans 3:19.) When we stand before the judgment seat of God, we won't be able to hand Him an excuse from our mothers or from anyone else and expect to be released from guilt. As Jesus put it, "They have no excuse for their sin" (John 15:22).

That's why Jesus came. He is our excuse. He is the note that gets us off the hook. When we believe in Him and follow Him as His disciples, we are released from our guilt. Christ stands with us at the judgment seat and says, "Please excuse _____. He/she belongs to Me." And that's okay with God.

Face the Music

Have you ever heard the expression "Face the music"? Here's how that phrase came about:

Many years ago, a man wanted to play in the Imperial Orchestra, but he couldn't play a note. Since he was a person of great wealth and influence, however, he demanded to be allowed to join the orchestra so that he could perform in front of the king.

The conductor agreed to let him sit in the second row of the orchestra. Even though he couldn't read music, he was given a flute, and when a concert would begin, he would raise his instrument, pucker his lips, and move his fingers. He went through all the motions of playing, but he never made a sound.

This deception went on for two years. Then one day a new conductor took over the Imperial Orchestra. He told the orchestra that he wanted to personally audition all the players to see how well they could play. The audition would weed out all those who weren't able to meet his standards, and he would dismiss them from the orchestra.

One by one the players performed in his presence. Frantic with worry when it was his turn, the phony flutist pretended to be sick. The doctor who was ordered to examine him, however, declared that he was perfectly well. The conductor insisted that the man appear and demonstrate his skill.

Shamefacedly, the man had to confess that he was a fake. That was the day he had to "face the music."

✔ Application:

Many of us go through the motions of the Christian life. We attend church or youth group, recite Bible verses, and say all the right things. In reality, though, we are fakes. A time is coming when all of us will be called to stand before the judge of heaven and earth and "face the music." No one will be able to hide in the crowd. The phonies will be separated from the true players. (See Matthew 12:36-37 and 25:31-46.)

Finish the Race

The Barcelona Olympics of 1992 provided one of track and field's most incredible moments.

Britain's Derek Redmond had dreamed all his life of winning a gold medal in the 400-meter race, and his dream was in sight as the gun sounded in the semifinals at Barcelona. He was running the race of his life and could see the finish line as he rounded the turn into the backstretch. Suddenly he felt a sharp pain go up the back of his leg. He fell face first onto the track with a torn right hamstring.

Sports Illustrated recorded the dramatic events:

As the medical attendants were approaching, Redmond fought to his feet. "It was animal instinct," he would say later. He set out hopping, in a crazed attempt to finish the race. When he reached the stretch, a large man in a T-shirt came out of the stands, hurled aside a security guard and ran to Redmond, embracing him. It was Jim Redmond, Derek's father. "You don't have to do this," he told his weeping son. "Yes, I do," said Derek. "Well, then," said Jim, "we're going to finish this together."

And they did. Fighting off security men, the son's head sometimes buried in his father's shoulder, they stayed in Derek's lane all the way to the end, as the crowd gaped, then rose and howled and wept.

Derek didn't walk away with the gold medal, but he walked away with an incredible memory of a father who, when he saw his son in pain, left his seat in the stands to help him finish the race.

☑ Application:

That's what God does for us. When we are experiencing pain and we're struggling to finish the race, we can be confident that we have a loving Father who won't let us do it alone. He left His place in heaven to come alongside us in the person of His Son, Jesus Christ. "I am with you always," says Jesus, "to the very end of the age" (Matt. 28:20).

The Flying V

Ever wonder why geese fly in a V formation? Scientists at Cal Tech did. They put their computers and flight simulators to work and discovered the answer—flocks of geese form this pattern because it's the easiest way to fly.

The formation acts aerodynamically like a single wing; that is, wind drag is distributed equally across all the birds. This in turn reduces drag on each individual bird. Twenty-five geese flying together in a V can travel seventy percent farther than one goose flying alone.

Because the lead goose actually situates itself slightly behind the perfect point position of the V, the geese that follow relieve some of its wind drag. It does not have to work harder than the others.

The benefit of the air flow pattern in the V (because it acts as a single flying wing) goes both ways. While the lead birds pull along those that are behind, the followers' flight sends relief back up to the front.

☑ Application:

From geese we can learn that, although we live in a society that promotes individualism and self-reliance, we function more effectively in community. Like the geese, we were created by God to work together, serve together, and encourage and support each other. When we cooperate and help each other to succeed, we not only accomplish much, but we do it with less stress and difficulty. Let's do it God's way.

The Flying Wallendas

The climactic event at Detroit's Cobo Hall exhibition of Ringling Brothers Barnum and Bailey Circus was the high-wire act of the Wallenda family, or the Flying Wallendas, as they were known. They were among the greatest tightwire walkers in all of circus history.

One of their acts was walking the tightrope in the formation of a four-level pyramid. Four or five men formed the first level, two or three men made up the second level, two more were on the third, and finally a little girl topped the pyramid. Maintaining this four-level pyramid, they would make their way across the tightrope from one side of the arena to the other. It was incredible and unprecedented. They did it night after night, month after month around the world.

One particular evening, as the show came to its conclusion, the four-level pyramid was about to start. The audience tensed in anticipation, sitting in total silence in the dark arena. The spotlights picked the Wallendas out of the air as they started moving across the wire. About two-thirds of the way across, however, one of the men on the first level, young Dede Wallenda, began to tremble in his knees. He cried out in German, "I cannot hold on any longer!" With that, he crumbled, and the entire pyramid collapsed. Several of the Wallendas fell to the floor many feet below. Some were crippled for life and one died.

☑ Application:

Have you ever felt like Dede Wallenda? The pressures of school, homework, parents, family, or friends weigh down on you until you feel like yelling, "Help! I cannot hold on any longer!" While facing those times, we need to surround ourselves with loving friends and hold on to Christ. That's what the church is all about. The church doesn't exist to put additional pressure on us, but to support us and provide us with the help we need to survive in the world.

When you feel like your knees are about to buckle, come to Christ. Come to His people, the church. "Come to me, all you who are weary and burdened, and I will give you rest" (Matt. 11:28).

Footprints in the Sand

A story is told about a man who dreamed he was at the end of his life. He saw his life as if it were a walk along a beach with Jesus. As he looked back over his life he saw two sets of footprints in the sand along most of the way—one set belonging to him, the other to Jesus. He noticed, though, that many times along the path of his life there was only one set of footprints in the sand. He also noticed that it happened at the very lowest and saddest times in his life.

This really bothered the man, and he questioned the Lord about it. "Lord, You said that You would never leave me nor forsake me. You said that once I decided to follow You, You'd walk with me all the way. But I have noticed that during the most difficult times in my life, there was only one set of footprints. I don't understand why, when I needed You most, You would leave me."

Jesus replied, "My son, I want you to know that I love you and that I would never leave you. Look again at those footprints. During your times of trouble and suffering, the footprints you saw were Mine. I was carrying you."

☑ Application:

We can be certain that when we are going through the difficult times of life, God is always with us. Never doubt His presence, even though you can't feel Him or see Him at the time. He keeps His word: "Never will I leave you; never will I forsake you" (Heb. 13:5).

France 1943

A crowd of men, women, and children huddled together at the train station. Dressed for a long journey and standing with their bags at their sides, they spoke in low tones. Armed men in the grim uniform of the SS, the feared wing of the Nazi army, surrounded the travelers.

The people shivering on the platform were not criminals. They were Jews, French Jews who had been hauled from their homes by the occupying soldiers and French Nazi sympathizers.

The non-Jewish French watched these events unfold with increasing concern. After all, these people were neighbors and friends. The group included the watchmaker and his family, the lad who sold newspapers, the old lady who made beautiful quilts. Now they were being "relocated."

The plumes of smoke could be seen even before the train was heard. The townspeople cast a nervous eye toward the train platform as the black, soot-belching locomotive ground to a halt.

Armed guards herded the Jews into the train cars. They went cooperatively, putting up no resistance. Concerned observers wondered why this was taking place; but they told themselves that things would be fine, that there was no need to worry about these friends and neighbors. They were in good hands.

How could they believe that? Because neatly printed in French on the door of every boxcar was the reassuring logo "Charitable Transport Company."

☑ Application:

We, too, are lulled into apathy or deceived into inactivity by the sloganeering of the world. Docilely we are led to our destruction. Take television, for example. How could something so entertaining be dangerous? Though it seems harmless—even good—it presents a value system that undermines the sanctity of marriage, families, morality, the church, respect for life, and the Gospel of Christ. Just another innocent-looking boxcar, like those that took millions of Jews to the gas chambers.

"Be self-controlled and alert. Your enemy the devil prowls around like a roaring lion looking for someone to devour" (I Peter 5:8).

Getting the Word Out

A legend recounts the return of Jesus to heaven after His time on earth. He returned bearing the marks of His earthly pilgrimage with its cruel cross and shameful death.

The angel Gabriel approached Him and said, "Master, You must have suffered terribly for people down there."

"I did," said Jesus.

"And," continued Gabriel, "do they now know all about how You loved them and what You did for them?"

"Oh, no," said Jesus. "Not yet. Right now, only a handful of people in Palestine know."

Gabriel was perplexed. "Then what have You done," he asked, "to let all people know about Your love for them?"

"Well, I've asked Peter, James, John, and a few others to tell people about Me. Those who are told will in turn tell others, and the Gospel will be spread to the farthest reaches of the globe. Ultimately, all of humankind will hear about Me and what I have done on their behalf."

Gabriel frowned and looked skeptical. He knew that people weren't dependable. "Yes," he said, "but what if Peter and James and John grow weary? What if the people who come after them forget? And what if, way down in the twentieth and twenty-first centuries, people get too busy to bother telling others about You? Haven't You made any other plans?"

"No, I've made no other plans, Gabriel," Jesus answered. "I'm counting on them."

☑ Application:

It's been said that the Christian faith is only one generation away from extinction. That's because with each generation comes the renewed responsibility to take the good news of the Gospel to the world. Are you doing your part? "Therefore go and make disciples of all nations, baptizing them in the name of the Father and of the Son and of the Holy Spirit" (Matt. 28:19).

The Glove

(Best presented as an object lesson, this illustration needs only a glove.)

Amazingly, a glove can do all sorts of things—pick up a book, wave good-bye, scratch my head, pat someone on the back, or slap somebody in the face. (Put a glove on your hand and demonstrate how the "glove" can do these or other similar things.)

This glove can do nothing if I take my hand out of it, however. (Demonstrate this.) All it does is lie there. I can yell at it, get mad at it, try to teach it lessons, but to no avail. It can do nothing on its own. Without my hand inside, the glove is nothing more than an ordinary piece of cloth (or leather or whatever it's made of).

☑ Application:

People, like this glove, can do little of real consequence on their own. In the flesh we are weak, but with Christ we are strong. When my hand is inside the glove, the glove can do anything my hand wants it to do. In Philippians 4:13, Paul teaches me that I am like a glove. On my own I can do nothing. But with Christ in me, I can do whatever Christ wants me to do. He is the one who gives me the strength and the ability to do it. We can be sure that if we obey Christ, He will be with us and give us the strength to do His will.

The Greatest Hitter in the World

A little boy was overheard talking to himself as he strutted through the backyard, wearing his baseball cap and toting a ball and bat. "I'm the greatest hitter in the world," he announced. Then he tossed the ball into the air, swung at it, and missed. "Strike One!" he yelled. Undaunted, he picked up the ball and said again, "I'm the greatest hitter in the world!" He tossed the ball into the air. When it came down, he swung again and missed. "Strike Two!" he cried.

The boy then paused a moment to examine his bat and ball carefully.

He spit on his hands and rubbed them together. He straightened his cap and said once more, "I'm the greatest hitter in the world!" Again he tossed the ball up in the air and swung at it. He missed. "Strike Three! Wow!" the boy exclaimed. "I'm the greatest pitcher in the world!"

☑ Application:

Your attitude determines how circumstances impact your life. The little boy's circumstances hadn't changed, but his optimistic attitude prompted him to give an encouraging meaning to what had happened.

What difficult time are you going through right now? Can you do something to change it? If you can, don't wait another day—make the needed changes. If you can't change the circumstance, however, change your attitude—you'll discover that circumstances won't have the last word.

The Greyhound Races

Greyhound racing, a popular betting sport in some parts of the country, attracts crowds who enjoy watching incredibly sleek and beautiful dogs run as fast as they can around a track. Unlike race horses, greyhounds run without the assistance of a jockey. To keep the dogs running in the right direction, they are trained to chase a mechanical rabbit made of fur as it zips along the track in front of them. A man in the press box electronically controls the speed of the rabbit, keeping the rabbit just out in front of the dogs. The dogs never catch up to it.

At a Florida track some years back, a big race was about to begin. The dogs crouched in their cages, ready to go, while betting spectators finished placing their wagers. At the proper moment, the gun went off. The man in the press box pushed his lever, starting the rabbit down the first stretch, while the cage doors flew open, releasing the dogs to take off after the little rabbit. As the rabbit made the first turn, however, an electrical short in the system caused the rabbit to come to a complete stop, to explode, and to go up in flames. Poof! All that was left was a bit of black stuff hanging on the end of a wire.

Their rabbit gone, the bewildered dogs didn't know how to act. According to news reports, several dogs simply stopped running and laid down on the track, their tongues hanging out. Two dogs, still frenzied with the chase, ran into a wall, breaking several ribs. Another dog began chasing his tail, while the rest howled at the people in the stands.

Not one dog finished the race.

✔ Application:

Like racing greyhounds, people pursue their chosen rabbit. Humans need some reason for living—for running the race. What is your goal, your purpose in life, your hope? What if it were taken away? Sadly, many young people chase an illusion, a mechanical rabbit of sorts, that ultimately turns out to offer no hope at all.

Paul the apostle wrote out what kept him motivated to run the race: "For to me, to live is Christ"(Phil. 1:21). Jesus is the only one who can give us lasting purpose, meaning, and hope. Paul later wrote, "I press on toward the goal to win the prize for which God has called me heavenward in Christ Jesus" (Phil. 3:14). To know Christ is the only lasting, eternal goal.

The Grocery Store Clerk

Jim Davis, a grocery store clerk who loves his job, prides himself on his good work. One of his pet peeves is out-of-control toddlers and parents who yell at their kids but do nothing to correct their children's obnoxious behavior.

One evening, Jim was checking out a customer who had a shopping cart full of groceries. While ringing up the sale, a child behind him began screaming very loudly, and an angry man responded by shouting, "Get down!"

What a jerk, thought Jim, without even looking up. He kept on calling out prices and moving the groceries past the scanner. The kid behind him was still crying, and again he heard the man yell, "Get down!" *Sheesh. Talk about poor parenting,* thought Jim. *This guy is a total jerk.* He kept on checking groceries without looking up.

Finally finishing the customer's cart, Jim looked up and said, "That'll be $89.95, ma'am." Seeing no one, he looked around and noticed that everyone, including his customer, was lying face down on the floor.

He turned around just in time to see a gunman leave the store. The checker behind him, still lying on the floor, calmly said, "Jim, you know the second time you heard 'Get down,' his gun was pointed right at your head."

☑ Application:

We can get so accustomed to the noise of our culture and the distractions of the world that when we hear someone telling us something important, we blow it off as if it were of no significance. How many times has a parent, a teacher, or a youth leader warned you about the dangers of abusing drugs and alcohol or of doing other behaviors that can kill you? We hear so much of that, we sometimes ignore the messengers, assuming the warning is meant for someone else. We go on with business as usual.

You put yourself at great risk when you blow off an important message, one that can save your life. The time will come when there'll be no more opportunities to act on the message. "Now is the day of salvation" (II Cor. 6:2).

Hannibal's Fire

In 218 B.C. the Carthaginian king, Hannibal, stood atop the lofty Col de la Traversette pass in the Alps and looked down upon the mighty Roman Empire, the kingdom he had come to destroy.

Inflamed with hatred, he drove his tattered army down the mountainside. Before his quest for glory could be realized, however, he had to overcome the last obstacle blocking his path—an enormous rock, wedged into the valley floor, that prevented his passage. It was impossible to move his chariots and wagons through the pass unless the rock was dislodged and moved out of the way.

Attempts to crack the rock with picks and hammers failed. Sacrifices and incantations likewise produced no results. Desperate and impatient,

Hannibal cried out, "Burn it!" To his half-dead troops, this irrational command seemed mad. Surely Hannibal wasn't serious.

Nevertheless, within a few hours felled trees were clustered around the rock to fuel the fire that Hannibal had commanded. When the wood was laid, the soldiers lit the fire and watched in fascination as the flames formed an inferno around the rock. Finally, unable to withstand the heat, the rock yielded with a deafening "CRACK!" heard down the valley. The impenetrable rock had split in two. Hannibal and his army descended upon Rome, and the course of world history was changed forever.

☑ Application:

Many people believe it's possible to change bad people into good people with education, an improved environment, increased economic assistance, or special programs. As helpful as those things may be, they are merely picks and hammers scratching an enormous rock. Only God is able to change the human heart. In one sense, when we spread the good news of the Gospel of Christ (or when we serve others in the name of Christ), we lay around the hearts of people firewood to be lit by the power of the Holy Spirit for the purpose of changing people from the inside out.

The Hermit's Gift

There was once an old monastery that had fallen upon hard times. Centuries earlier, it had been a thriving monastery where many dedicated monks lived and worked and had great influence on the realm. But now only five monks lived there, and they were all over seventy years old. This was clearly a dying order.

A few miles from the monastery lived an old hermit who many thought was a prophet. One day as the monks agonized over the impending demise of their order, they decided to visit the hermit to see if he might have some advice for them. Perhaps he would be able to see the future and show them what they could do to save the monastery.

The hermit welcomed the five monks to his hut, but when they explained the purpose of their visit, the hermit could only commiserate with them. "Yes, I understand how it is," said the hermit. "The spirit has gone out of the people. Hardly anyone cares much for the old things anymore."

"Is there anything you can tell us," the abbot inquired of the hermit, "that would help us save the monastery?"

"No, I'm sorry," said the hermit. "I don't know how your monastery can be saved. The only thing that I can tell you is that one of you is an apostle of God."

The monks were both disappointed and confused by the hermit's cryptic statement. They returned to the monastery, wondering what the hermit could have meant by the statement, "One of you is an apostle of God." For months after their visit, the monks pondered the significance of the hermit's words.

"One of us is an apostle of God," they mused. "Did he actually mean one of us monks here at the monastery? That's impossible. We are all too old. We are too insignificant. On the other hand, what if it's true? And if it is true, then which one of us is it? Do you suppose he meant the abbot? Yes, if he meant anyone, he probably meant the abbot. He has been our leader for more than a generation. On the other hand, he might have meant Brother Thomas. Certainly Brother Thomas is a holy man—a man of wisdom and light. He couldn't have meant Brother Elred. Elred gets crotchety at times and is difficult to reason with. On the other hand, he is almost always right. Maybe the hermit did mean Brother Elred. But surely he could not have meant Brother Phillip. Phillip is so passive, so shy—a real nobody. Still, he's always there when you need him. He's loyal and trustworthy. Yes, he could have meant Phillip. Of course, the hermit didn't mean me. He couldn't possibly have meant me. I'm just an ordinary person. Yet, suppose he did? Suppose I am an apostle of God? Oh God, not me. I couldn't be that much for you. Or could I?"

As they contemplated in this manner, the old monks began to treat each other with extraordinary respect on the off chance that one of them might actually be an apostle of God. And on the off, off chance that each monk himself might be the apostle spoken of by the hermit, each monk began to treat himself with extraordinary respect.

Because the monastery was situated in a beautiful forest, many people came there to picnic on its tiny lawn and to walk on its paths, and even now and then to go into the tiny chapel to meditate. As they did so, without even being conscious of it, they sensed the aura of extraordinary respect that now began to surround the five old monks and seemed to radiate out of them, permeating the atmosphere of the place. There was something strangely attractive, even compelling, about it. Hardly knowing why, people began to come back to the monastery more frequently to picnic, to play, to pray. They began to bring their friends to show them this special place. And their friends brought their friends.

As more and more visitors came, some of the younger men started to talk with the old monks. After a while one asked if he could join them. Then another. And another. Within a few years the monastery had once again become a thriving order and, thanks to the hermit's gift, a vibrant center of light and spirituality throughout the realm.

(Adapted from M. Scott Peck, *The Different Drum*, Simon & Schuster, 1988.)

☑ Application:

Sometimes, just like the old monks, we ask, "How can we attract more kids to our youth group? How can we get some new life in here and grow, both numerically and spiritually?" Perhaps the answer has to do with how we regard each other. How do we treat each other? Are we always putting each other down and creating an atmosphere of criticism and negativism? Or are we treating each other with extraordinary dignity and respect?

John 17 records Jesus' prayer to His Father for the church—for you and me. He asked that all of us would be one so that the world might believe. When we care for each other and treat each other with love and respect, then those in the world find the church to be attractive, even compelling. Let's stop fighting and hurting each other and be one body in Christ.

The Hopeless Baseball Game

Recently the San Diego Padres played the San Francisco Giants (substitute your favorite baseball teams here) at the stadium. I took my son to the game, expecting to have a good time. We turned in our tickets at the gate, bought hot dogs, drinks, peanuts, popcorn, Cracker Jacks, and a program, and sat down in our seats right on the first-base line. We were all set to watch a good game.

At the top of the first inning, though, the Padres' pitcher walked a batter. He followed that act by walking a second batter. He hit the third batter with a pitch, loading the bases. He pitched the next batter a home run—a grand slam. Unfortunately (as we soon discovered), the manager left the pitcher in, and he proceeded to walk two more players. Finally, the pitcher was replaced with a new guy, and bingo! The next batter hit a triple, scoring two more runs. By the time the inning was over, the Giants were ahead seven to zero.

Unable to do anything in the bottom of the first, the Padres quickly returned to the outfield. Things went from bad to ugly. To make a long story short, before the second inning was over, the score was fourteen–zip.

The players knew it, and we knew it—the game was over. We hadn't even had a chance to eat our hot dogs. Some spectators hadn't even arrived yet. But the game was over. There was no way the Padres could come back from fourteen to nothing.

The players looked discouraged. Angry fans were booing and throwing things. People started to leave the stadium. What a disaster.

Chomping into my hot dog, I set out on a crazy line of thought: What if by some magic I could return the game to the score zero to zero—right now in the second inning? With that kind of score, the players would be hopeful once again. Their optimism would motivate them to play with intensity. The resulting competition would allow the fans to be happily hoping their team would win. The game would once again be exciting and interesting—and we could finish eating all this junk food.

☑ Application:

Starting the score over in a bad second inning is the way forgiveness works. Forgiveness restores our hope. Many people feel hopelessly weighed down by sin. Things have gotten out of hand. They're losing so badly that they feel their life is as good as over. People who feel that way often take their own lives.

The Gospel does a miraculous thing, though. Even given a hopeless score that clearly shows that Satan is winning, Jesus is able to make the game zero to zero again. When our sins are forgiven, we have a clean start; it's a whole new ball game. Once again we have hope.

How to Catch a Monkey

Native hunters in the jungles of Africa have a clever way of trapping monkeys.

They slice a coconut in two, hollow it out, and in one half of the shell cut a hole just big enough for a monkey's hand to pass through. Then they place an orange in the other coconut half before fastening together the two halves of the coconut shell. Finally, they secure the coconut to a tree with a rope, retreat into the jungle, and wait.

Sooner or later, an unsuspecting monkey swings by, smells the delicious orange, and discovers its location inside the coconut. The monkey then slips his hand through the small hole, grasps the orange, and tries to pull it through the hole. Of course, the orange won't come out; it's too big for the hole. To no avail the persistent monkey continues to pull and pull, never realizing the danger he is in.

While the monkey struggles with the orange, the hunters simply stroll in and capture the monkey by throwing a net over him. As long as the monkey keeps his fist wrapped around the orange, the monkey is trapped.

✔ Application:

It's too bad—the poor monkey could save its own life if it would only let go of the orange. It rarely occurs to a monkey, however, that it can't have both the orange and its freedom. That delicious orange becomes a deadly trap.

The world sets traps for you that are not unlike the monkey trap. You hear constantly that if you just have enough money, enough stuff, enough power, enough prestige—then you'll be happy. Under that illusion people spend their whole lives trying to pull the orange out of the coconut. Don't fall for it. Don't be trapped by thinking you must have it all. What the world offers appears delicious, but it eventually robs us of our freedom, our happiness, even our lives.

Jesus said, "Do not store up for yourselves treasures on earth, where moth and rust destroy, and where thieves break in and steal. But store up for yourselves treasures in heaven" (Matt. 6:19, 20). Jesus also said "What good is it for a man to gain the whole world, yet forfeit his soul?" (Mark 8:36).

The Insurance Claim

A man injured on the job filed an insurance claim. The insurance company requested more information, so the man wrote the insurance company the following letter of explanation:

Dear Sirs:

I am writing in response to your request concerning clarification of the information I supplied in block #11 on the insurance form, which asked for the cause of the injury. I answered, "Trying to do the job alone." I trust that the following explanation will be sufficient.

I am a bricklayer by trade. On the date of the injury, I was working alone, laying brick around the top of a three-story building. When I finished the job, I had about five hundred pounds of brick left over. Rather than carry the bricks down by hand, I decided to put them into a barrel and lower them by a pulley that was fastened to the top of the building.

I secured the end of the rope at ground level, went back up to the top of the building, loaded the bricks into the barrel, and pushed it over the side. I then went back down to the ground and untied the rope, holding it securely to insure the slow descent of the barrel. As you will note in block #6 of the insurance form, I weigh 145 pounds. At the shock of being jerked off the ground so swiftly by the five hundred pounds of bricks in the barrel, I lost my presence of mind and forgot to let go of the rope.

Between the second and third floors I met the barrel. This accounts for the bruises and lacerations on my upper body. Fortunately, I retained enough presence of mind to maintain my tight hold on the rope and proceeded rapidly up the side of the building, not stopping until my right hand was jammed in the pulley. This accounts for my broken thumb (see block #4). Despite the pain, I continued to hold tightly to the rope. Unfortunately, at approximately the same time, the barrel hit the ground and the bottom fell out of the barrel. Devoid of the weight of the bricks, the barrel now weighed about fifty pounds. I again refer you to block #6, where my weight is listed. I began a rapid descent.

In the vicinity of the second floor, I met the barrel coming up. This explains the injury to my legs and lower body. Slowed only slightly, I continued my descent, landing on the pile of bricks. Fortunately, my back was only sprained. I am sorry to report, however, that at this point I again lost my presence of mind—and let go of the rope.

I trust that this answers your concern. Please note that I am finished trying to do the job alone.

☑ Application:

The Christian life is not easy to live "on your own." You need people who stand beside you to support you and help you to succeed. That's why God created the church. There are no Lone Rangers in the family of God. We really do need each other. We are a community, a family of faith, and when we all work together, we can accomplish great things for Christ. (See I Corinthians 12.)

Jesus and the Football Team

At a high school summer camp, a mere two weeks before football "hell week," as the players called preseason training, several members of the varsity football team made decisions to follow Christ in response to the camp speaker's inspirational talk about Jesus turning losers into winners. The next Sunday morning, those players all showed up for church.

"Great to see you here," said the pastor when he greeted the boys after the service.

"Yeah, well, we all became Christians," said one of the boys.

"Because with Jesus on our team, we can't lose!" said another.

"Well, I'm very happy for you," grinned the pastor.

The following Saturday night, one of the girls in the youth group noticed one of the football players standing in front of a neighbor's house. A party was in full swing, and the boy was staggering around on the lawn, apparently drunk. She saw him urinate on a friend's parked car.

"What are you doing here?" she questioned. "I thought you became a Christian?" He snapped back, "Hey, that doesn't mean I can't have fun! I'm not going to let Jesus or anybody else tell me what to do!"

During the course of the season, the football team lost seven of their first eight games. Apparently, Jesus forgot to suit up. One by one the players who "became Christians" quit showing up for church and youth group activities. By the end of the season, it was hard to find a single player within ten miles of the church on Sunday morning.

☑ Application:

Yes, Jesus can turn losers into winners, but not winners according to the way the world defines winning. Jesus said that the only way to win is to lose. (See Matthew 16:25.) Jesus Himself lost His own life in order to achieve victory over sin and death. He is the ultimate winner, but He won by paying a high price. Jesus is our example; He calls us to become His disciples and follow Him in costly obedience. If you are following Christ for selfish reasons and are unwilling to conform your life to His, you will lose. On the other hand, if you are ready to lose your life for His sake, you will ultimately win. Faith without obedience is no faith at all. (See James 2:17.)

The Jewelry Store Caper

(This story is attributed to the philosopher Søren Kierkegaard.)

One night, a group of thieves broke into a jewelry store. But rather than stealing anything, they simply switched all the price tags. The next day no one could tell what was valuable and what was cheap. The expensive jewels had suddenly become cheap, and the costume jewelry, which had been virtually worthless before, was suddenly of great value. Customers who thought they were purchasing valuable gems were getting fakes. Those who couldn't afford the higher priced items were leaving the store with treasures.

✓ Application:

In our world someone came in and switched all the price tags. It's hard to tell what is of value and what is not. Great value is given to the accumulation of material wealth and the power that goes with it. The world puts a high price on popularity, prestige, beauty, and fame. But Jesus taught that such things are virtually worthless in the only "jewelry store" that matters: the kingdom of God. "Do not store up for yourselves treasures on earth, where moth and rust destroy, and where thieves break in and steal. But store up for yourselves treasures in heaven, where moth and rust do not destroy, and where thieves do not break in and steal" (Matt. 6:19, 20).

The Jigsaw Puzzle

A family had a hobby of putting together jigsaw puzzles. The father regularly brought home puzzles of greater and greater difficulty. One night he presented his family with a puzzle of over one thousand pieces. Immediately they tackled it. After an hour, however, the family was frustrated. No matter how hard they tried, they couldn't get the puzzle started.

The father then discovered that he had accidently switched the box top with the top from another puzzle. The picture they were looking at wasn't the puzzle they were working on.

☑ Application:

We may feel frustrated with God because He doesn't live up to the expectations we have of Him. Sometimes we feel frustrated with the church because it doesn't match up with the ideal church that we have in mind. We're often frustrated with others because they fall short of expectations that we have of them.

Perhaps we should consider whether the problem in all these cases is that we are basing our expectations on a distorted view—of God or of the church or of others. Perhaps our expectations are unrealistic and can never be realized because we've been looking at the picture on the wrong box top.

We may also feel frustrated with ourselves because we don't believe we live up to what others want from us or even what we think God wants from us. More often than not, though, our problem is trying to make ourselves into someone else's image or change ourselves to fit someone else's standards for us. God created us each to be different. We all have our own "box-top picture," and the only way we can ever be successful in life is to be ourselves, allowing God to use us just the way we are.

The Job Applicant

Back when the telegraph was the fastest method of long-distance communication, a young man applied for a job as a Morse Code operator. Answering an ad in the newspaper, he went to the office address that was listed. When he arrived, he entered a large, busy office filled with noise and clatter, including the sound of the telegraph in the background. A sign on the receptionist's counter instructed job applicants to fill out a form and wait until they were summoned to enter the inner office.

The young man filled out his form and sat down with the seven other applicants in the waiting area. After a few minutes, the young man stood up, crossed the room to the door of the inner office, and walked right in. Naturally the other applicants perked up, wondering what was going on. They muttered among themselves that they hadn't heard any summons yet. They assumed that the young man who went into the office made a mistake and would be disqualified.

Within a few minutes, however, the employer escorted the young man out of the office and said to the other applicants, "Gentlemen, thank you very much for coming, but the job has just been filled."

The other applicants began grumbling to each other, and one spoke up saying, "Wait a minute, I don't understand. He was the last to come in, and we never even got a chance to be interviewed. Yet he got the job. That's not fair!"

The employer said, "I'm sorry, but all the time you've been sitting here, the telegraph has been ticking out the following message in Morse Code: 'If you understand this message, then come right in. The job is yours.' None of you heard it or understood it. This young man did. The job is his."

☑ Application:

We live in a world that is full of busyness and clatter, like that office. People are distracted and unable to hear the still, small voice of God as He speaks in creation, in the Scriptures, or in the life and work of Jesus Christ. Are you tuned in to God's voice? Do you hear Him when He speaks to you? Are you listening? "This is my Son, whom I love . . . Listen to him!" (Matt. 17:5).

The Kebbitch Itch

There is an old Hasidic tale about a woman whose name was Anna Kebbitch. She was a complainer. All day long she complained:

"I have so little money, my clothes are like old rags."

"My health is so bad, my back feels like the walls of Jericho."

"I must walk so far to draw water, my feet are like watermelons."

"My house is so small, I can barely move in it."

"My children visit me so little that they hardly know me."

One day, Anna Kebbitch woke up with an itch on her nose. All day long her nose itched. She went into town to visit the rabbi.

When the rabbi saw Anna, he asked her, "How are you, Anna?"

Anna replied, "I have so little money, my clothes are like old rags. My health is so bad, my back feels like the walls of Jericho. I must walk so far to draw water, my feet are like watermelons. My house is so small, I can barely move in it. My children visit me so little that they hardly know me. And now I have this itch on my nose and it plagues me so. Tell me, Rabbi, what does it mean?"

The rabbi said, "Anna, your itch is the Kebbitch Itch—the 'complainer's itch.' Its meaning is this: However you consider yourself, so shall you be."

The next morning, Anna woke up and her nose was still itching. She could barely move. Her back had turned to stone like the walls of Jericho. When she looked about her, she noticed that her house had shrunk until her arms stuck out the windows and her legs hung out the front door. She could not move in it. On the end of her legs were two huge watermelons. Her clothes had turned to old rags. When her son and daughter came walking by, Anna called out to them, but they continued walking on, wagging their heads—they didn't know her.

And her nose continued to itch.

In despair Anna remembered the meaning of the Kebbitch Itch: *However you consider yourself, so shall you be. What does this mean?*

Anna began to think: *You know, I do have money enough to live on and more. Henceforth, I will give out of my abundance to those who are not so well off. My health is not so bad. Actually, for someone my age, I feel quite well. I'm glad I have such a nice house to live in. It's not large, but it's comfortable and quite warm. I really don't mind my walk to draw water. I love to smell the flowers along the path. And my children—I'm so proud that they have become independent and are now able to take care of themselves.*

Miraculously, while Anna was saying these things, her situation returned to normal—and her outlook on life changed forever. When the rabbis tell Anna's story, they end with this statement: May your noses itch forever.

☑ Application:

We may not get the Kebbitch itch, but we need to be reminded that our outlook affects outcomes. Our attitude makes a difference. Do you complain all the time? Do you expect the worst in others? Do you always resent it when other people have more than you or seem to be doing better than you? The result of that kind of thinking is this: your situation will probably get worse.

On the other hand, if you are a positive person who sees the good in others, rejoices with others who are doing better than you, and praises God for all that He has given to you, remember this: your situation will probably get better.

Christians are to be positive people. We have every reason to be.

The Kiss

In his book *Mortal Lessons* (Touchstone Books, 1987) physician Richard Selzer describes a scene in a hospital room after he had performed surgery on a young woman's face:

I stand by the bed where the young woman lies . . . her face, postoperative. . . her mouth twisted in palsy . . . clownish. A tiny twig of the facial nerve, one of the muscles of her mouth, has been severed. She will be that way from now on. I had followed with religious fervor the curve of her flesh, I promise you that. Nevertheless, to remove the tumor in her cheek, I had cut this little nerve. Her young husband is in the room. He stands on the opposite side of the bed, and together they seem to be in a world all their own in the evening lamplight . . . isolated from me . . .

private.

Who are they? I ask myself . . . he and this wry mouth I have made, who gaze at and touch each other so generously. The young woman speaks. "Will my mouth always be like this?" she asks. "Yes," I say, "it will. It is because the nerve was cut." She nods and is silent. But the young man smiles. "I like it," he says. "It's kind of cute."

All at once I know who he is. I understand, and I lower my gaze. One is not bold in an encounter with the divine. Unmindful, he bends to kiss her crooked mouth, and I am so close I can see how he twists his own lips to accommodate to hers . . . to show her that their kiss still works."

☑ Application:

God accommodated Himself to us by coming down from heaven as a little baby. He came to us, and then He allowed His body to be twisted on the cross to show us that the love of God still works. Regardless of the scars that you bear from the ravages of sin, you are loved by God. You are beautiful to Him. You were created in His image, and you bear the likeness of His Son. He will never stop loving you. "For God so loved the world that he gave his one and only Son" (John 3:16).

"Lambing" in New Zealand

The beautiful, green hills of New Zealand, a country known for its sheep industry, are dotted everywhere with white sheep. During the yearly lambing season, thousands of baby lambs are born. Unfortunately, some lambs die at birth. Many mother sheep are also lost during lambing season; they die giving birth. In an attempt to save the orphaned lambs, the shepherds match baby lambs who have lost their mothers with mother sheep who have lost their lambs. It's not as easy as it sounds, though—a mother sheep won't accept a lamb and nurse it unless it is her own.

How, then, do shepherds get a mother sheep to accept an orphaned lamb as her own? The process is as old as shepherding itself. The mother's own lamb, which has died, is skinned, and the skin of the dead lamb is draped over the living lamb as it is placed by the adoptive mother's side. The mother sheep then smells the skin and accepts the orphaned lamb as her own.

☑ Application:

Lambing season in New Zealand reminds us of what Jesus did for us on the cross. When John wrote in Revelation 7:14 and 12:11 of our being saved by "the blood of the Lamb," it was in terms that people in agrarian societies vividly understood.

Paul wrote to the Ephesians, "But now in Christ Jesus you who once were far away have been brought near through the blood of Christ. For he . . . has destroyed the barrier, the dividing wall of hostility . . ." (Eph. 2:13, 14). Because of Christ's blood, God accepts us as His own. Once we were orphans, but now we are God's adopted children.

Laying Bricks or Building Cathedrals

Christopher Wren, who designed St. Paul's Cathedral in London (one of the world's most beautiful buildings), wrote about the reactions of construction workers who were asked what they were doing. Those workers who were bored and tired responded by saying, "I'm laying bricks" or "I'm carrying stones."

But one worker, who was mixing cement, seemed cheerful and enthusiastic about his work. Asked what he was doing, he replied, "I'm building a magnificent cathedral."

Surveys have found that most people hate their work. They don't look forward to going to work; instead they are bored with it and weary of it. They dream of winning the state lottery so they never have to work another day in their lives.

God didn't create us to be bored and unfulfilled by our work. He created us to serve Him in everything we do, including our work. "Work" in Scripture is another word for "worship." God wants us to enjoy our work because our work is what brings glory to God. It's one way we worship God. Paul wrote that we should be happy in our work because we are not working for men, but for God. (See Colossians 3:23.) In another place he wrote, "Whatever you do, do it all for the glory of God" (I Cor. 10:31).

If you look at your work merely as something do to make a few bucks and survive, you won't be happy in your work. On the other hand, if you decide to glorify God in your work, you will not only be happy as you work, but God will meet all of your needs as well.

The Lifeboat

(This is based on a true story.)

Annie was a large, rather unattractive girl.

Actually, Annie was fat.

A member of a youth group, Annie regularly attended most of the youth functions and Bible studies. During one of those meetings, the youth leader introduced a situational learning game called, "The Lifeboat."

He instructed the dozen high school kids present to form their chairs to resemble the seating on a lifeboat. Then he said, "You twelve are the only survivors of a shipwreck. You have managed to make it to this lifeboat. Once you are aboard, however, you find to your horror that there are only provisions for eleven. Also, the boat can hold only eleven survivors. Twelve people will capsize the boat, leaving you all to drown. You must decide what to do."

The group stared blankly at each other for a few moments before bursting into lively discussion. They decided that for the good of the majority of the members of the group, one person must be sacrificed. But who?

As the group discussed who would be left to drown, they eliminated various individuals perceived to be of value to the survivors. The strongest and most athletic boys couldn't be sacrificed—their strength would be needed to row. Naturally, the boys wouldn't think of letting any of the pretty girls become shark food. Slowly each individual in the group, with the exception of Annie, was mentioned and then discarded as a candidate for sacrifice. Some were too smart, too talented, or too popular.

Finally, Annie, who may not have been attractive but who was not dumb, blurted out, "I'll jump."

"No, no!" protested the group. But when pressed, they couldn't think of one good reason why she shouldn't jump—so they remained silent.

When the time to play the game ran out, the group members announced that they couldn't reach a decision on what to do. The youth worker went on to teach a lesson using the example of the lifeboat. But Annie had already learned a lesson.

The next day, Annie jumped. Her youth group had affirmed her worst thoughts about herself. She truly was of no value.

Her "friends" in the youth group were baffled and deeply saddened by her suicide. After all, she had so much to live for. They just couldn't think of what it was.

☑ Application:

We rarely look below the surface to see in a person what Christ sees. Instead, we too often equate a person's value with his or her looks, popularity, possessions, or abilities. If none of those things is obvious, then we see no value at all in that individual.

"Man looks at the outward appearance, but the Lord looks at the heart" (I Sam. 16:7b; I Pet. 3:3, 4.) Christians need to see others as they are seen by God—as having inherent worth apart from what the world sees. Every human being was created in God's image and is loved by Him. Jesus died for all of us—and in Christ, we are all members of His family, brothers and sisters. Further, each one of us is gifted by His Holy Spirit to make a unique contribution to His kingdom. (See I Corinthians 12.)

What would you have said to Annie?

The Lifesaving Station

On a dangerous seacoast where shipwrecks often occur, there was once a crude little lifesaving station. The building was no more than a hut, and there was only one boat; but the few devoted members kept a constant watch over the sea. With no thought for themselves, they went out day and night, tirelessly searching for the lost. Some of those who were saved, and various others in the surrounding area, wanted to be associated with the station and give their time, money, and effort to support the work. New boats were bought and new crews trained. The little lifesaving station grew.

Some of these new members of the lifesaving station were unhappy that the building was so crude and poorly equipped. They felt that a more comfortable place should be provided as the first refuge of those who were saved from the sea. They replaced the emergency cots with beds and put better furniture in the enlarged building. Now the lifesaving station became a popular gathering place for its members, and they decorated it beautifully and furnished it exquisitely because they used it as sort of a club. Fewer members were now interested in going to sea on lifesaving missions, so they hired lifeboat crews to do this work. The lifesaving motif still prevailed in this club's decoration, and there was a memorial lifeboat in the room where the club initiations were held.

About this time a large ship was wrecked off the coast, and the hired crews brought in boatloads of cold, wet, half-drowned people. They were dirty and sick, and some of them were foreigners. The beautiful new club was in chaos. Immediately, the property committee hired someone to rig up a shower house outside the club, where victims of shipwrecks could be cleaned up before coming inside.

At the next meeting, there was a split in the club membership. Most of the members wanted to stop the club's lifesaving activities because they felt they were unpleasant and a hindrance to the normal social life of the club. A small number of members insisted upon lifesaving as their primary purpose and pointed out that they were still called a lifesaving station. The small group's members were voted down and told that if they wanted to save lives, they could begin their own lifesaving station down the coast.

They did.

As the years went by, however, the new station experienced the same changes that had occurred in the old station. It evolved into a club, and yet another lifesaving station was founded. History continued to repeat itself, and if you visit that seacoast today, you will find a number of exclusive clubs along that shore.

Shipwrecks are frequent in those waters, but most of the passengers drown.

☑ Application:

As disciples of Jesus, our primary task is to go and make disciples. (See Matthew 28:19.) To put it another way, we are to go and save lives. Unfortunately, we sometimes forget our purpose. We need to recover our passion for lifesaving. We need to be doers of the Word and not hearers only. (See James 1:22.)

The Little Girl and the Piano

A little girl wanted to become a great pianist, but all she could play on the piano was the simple little tune, "Chopsticks." No matter how hard she tried, that was the best she could do. Her parents decided after some time to arrange for a great maestro to teach her to play properly. Of course, the little girl was delighted.

When the little girl and her parents arrived at the maestro's mansion for the first lesson, they were escorted by the butler into the parlor, where they saw a beautiful concert grand piano. Immediately, the little girl dashed over to the piano and began playing "Chopsticks." Her embarrassed parents started across the room to tell her to stop, but as she played, the maestro entered the room and encouraged the little girl to continue.

The maestro then took a seat on the piano bench next to the little girl, listening to her play. After a moment he began to play along with her, adding

143

chords, runs, and arpeggios. The little girl continued to play "Chopsticks." The parents couldn't believe their ears. They were hearing a beautiful piano duet, played by their daughter and the maestro, and amazingly enough, the central theme of it was still "Chopsticks."

☑ Application:

At times you may feel like you're a nobody, that God can't use you to do great things. But think of that little girl. All she could play was "Chopsticks." Nobody wanted to hear "Chopsticks." It was an embarrassment to her parents and annoying to everyone else. Yet the maestro encouraged her to keep on playing.

God knows what you can do. He created you with gifts and talents. Sure, compared to some people's abilities, your gifts and talents may seem like "Chopsticks"—not very original and not very spectacular. But God says, "Keep on playing—and make some room on the piano bench for Me." God is able to take the little that we are able to do and turn it into something beautiful for Him.

The Long Jump

Imagine that you're out jogging one day with Mike, a world record holder in the long jump at twenty-nine feet, four inches. While you're running along, you hear a low rumble, and your feet sense a steadily increasing tremor that alerts you to the start of an earthquake like no other you've experienced.

Suddenly, a mere stride ahead of you and Mike, the earth splits open.

You both come to a full stop to discover that you are isolated on a small sliver of earth, separated from safety by a deep crevasse that is about thirty feet across. The little patch of earth you're standing on is crumbling in the continuing upheaval, and you see that it's a matter of moments before you both are cast into the crevasse where you'll be crushed by the lurching earth. Things look hopeless.

Your only hope is to jump across the canyon. Mike judges that the jump is about eight inches longer than his record-setting long jump, but he decides to try it anyway. He gets back as far as he can so that he can gather as much speed as possible. He crouches into a three-point stance, and you yell, "On your mark! Get set! GO!"

Mike runs as fast as he can. Right on the edge of the crevasse, he kicks off and launches himself into the air. It's a perfect jump. Sailing over the crevasse, he lands with the toes of both feet barely on the edge of the other side. His jump is an amazing twenty-nine feet, six inches—two inches farther than his world record! Unfortunately, the jump isn't far enough. His feet slip off the edge, and for a moment he scrambles to grab the edge with his hands. It's no good, though. As you watch he falls into the crevasse and dies. Poor Mike.

Now it's your turn. You crouch into a three-point stance as far from the take-off edge as possible. Mentally giving yourself the signal, you spring forward. Huffing and puffing, you pound up to the edge, kick off, and jump—straight down into the crevasse. You're dead too.

It didn't matter that Mike nearly got to the other side with a perfect, world-record long jump. It simply wasn't far enough. Judged by its final outcome, Mike's jump was no better than yours. Both of you died.

Getting to the heaven side of eternal life works much the same way. It doesn't matter how good you live, how many church services you attend, or how much better you are than other people. You can't save yourself. The best people in the world can't save themselves, "for all have sinned and fall short" (Rom. 3:23). No one is good enough on his or her own.

That's why Jesus came. He's the only one who ever lived a perfect life. When we put our faith and trust in Him and make Him Lord of our lives, His perfection becomes ours. He's the only one who can get us safely to the other side.

Lost Dog— $50 Reward

The following notice was spotted in the lost and found section of the newspaper:

LOST DOG—$50 REWARD Black and tan dog of poodle and German shepherd descent. Flea-bitten, left hind leg missing, no hair on rump, blind, and recently neutered. Answers to the name of "Lucky."

☑ Application:

Some of us are a lot like Lucky. Of mixed ancestry, not much to look at, and in pretty bad shape, we still answer to the name of Lucky. We are indeed fortunate, for like the dog, we have someone who cares enough about us to look for us, to pursue us, to desire us, to pay to get us back. And God did pay to get us back—it cost Him the life of His only Son. That dog is lucky, and so are we—lucky that our Master would love us so much.

Love, Julie

Mr. and Mrs. Jones received this letter from their daughter Julie, a college freshman:

Dear Mom and Dad,

I just thought I'd drop you a note to let you know what's going on with me. I've fallen in love with a guy named Blaze. He's a really neat guy, but he quit high school a few years ago to get married. That didn't work out, so he got a divorce last year. We've been going out for several weeks, and we're thinking about getting married in the fall. Until then, I've decided to move into his apartment. I think I might be pregnant. Oh yeah, I dropped out of school last week so that I could get a job to help support Blaze. I'm hoping I'll be able to finish college after we get married.

Mom and Dad, I just want you to know that everything I've written so far in this letter is a lie. None of it is true.

But Mom and Dad, it is true that I got a C in French and a D in Math. And it's also true that I need some more money. Could you please send me a hundred dollars? Thanks a bunch.

Love, Julie

She received a check in the mail from her parents two days later.

☑ Application:

Julie played it smart. She knew she could make bad news seem like good news if it were seen from a particular perspective.

Where do you get your perspective on life each day—from the Word of God or from MTV and the movies? We need to stay close to God and to His family, the church, or our perspective on life will become distorted, shaped by the values of the world.

When we stray away from the truth, we end up with a badly distorted view of reality. We aren't able to make good decisions or to know the difference between what is right and wrong, true and false. The good seems bad; the bad seems good. Our view of reality is always a matter of perspective, and the only perspective worth trusting is God's. Stay close to Him.

The Mirror

Once there was an old rich man with a cranky, miserable attitude. He visited a rabbi one day to see if the rabbi might be able to help him discover what was wrong with his life.

After the two men talked together for a while, the rabbi thought of a good way to illustrate to the rich man the problem with his life. Taking the man by the hand, he led him over to the window. He asked him to look out the window and tell him what he saw. The man stood there a moment before saying, "I see some men and women and a few children."

"Fine," said the rabbi. Once more he led the rich man by the hand across the room to the mirror. "Now look and tell me what you see."

The man frowned and said, "Well, obviously, I see myself."

"Interesting," the rabbi replied. "The window is made of glass, and the mirror is also made of glass. But the glass of the mirror has been covered with silver. As soon as you add the silver, you cease to see others and instead see only yourself."

☑ Application:

Like the old man, if you "cover your life with silver" (money, wealth), you'll be unhappy. Unhappiness overtakes you because you stop thinking of others, and you begin to think only of yourself. The way people feel happy is by loving God and loving others more than themselves. No one is more miserable than a vain, self-centered person.

A Night in the Haunted House

(As you tell this story, embellish it with as many creative details as you wish.)

One spooky Halloween night, a young man approached an old, abandoned house at the end of a deserted cul-de-sac. His friends had dared him to spend the night in this house that everyone knew was haunted. Tales of hauntings had been embellished over the years as kids repeated them at campfires and on late-night excursions. Whenever there was a full moon, they had heard, the three previous owners of the house, who had allegedly died gruesome and painful deaths, walked about inside the house, moaning out their anguish and plotting their revenge on the living.

That Halloween night, the young man cringed to see that the moon was indeed full.

Clutching his father's shotgun a little more tightly, he slung his bedroll and canteen through a broken window and entered the house. Finding his way through cobwebs and trash to the master bedroom, he laid out his bedroll next to the fireplace in the very spot where the owners gasped their last, terrified breaths.

Several hours passed, but he was unable to sleep. He had a strange feeling that someone else was in the house with him. He felt for his shotgun at his side. The reassurance was small compared to his growing sense that he was not alone.

At midnight he heard what sounded like footsteps. A few minutes later, he thought he heard something scratching on the walls. Who or what could it be? Forcing his panic down, he waited until the sounds stopped. The silence was no comfort, however, and as he grew more and more anxious, he began to sweat. Within a few minutes the scratching sound returned and was followed by a low, anguished moan. Ooooohhhhhhh.

Slowly and silently he lifted the shotgun from beside the bedroll. Clutching the gun tightly in his hands, he strained to see through the darkness what had caused him such mortal fear. The boarded up windows kept out all but the faintest reminder of moonlight.

Suddenly he saw them. Staring back at him from the foot of his bedroll were two hideous-looking eyes. Slowly he raised the barrel of the shotgun and tried to steady it with his trembling hands. BANG! (If you shout this, followed by a loud scream, the effect is great.)

What happened?

He accidentally shot off his big toe.

☑ Application:

Darkness keeps us from seeing clearly. Walking in the dark, it's easy to stumble and fall, to make bad decisions. We can end up shooting off our own toes.

Christ warned us about walking in darkness (Matt. 6:23), and offered to give us the light that we need. "I am the light of the world," He said. "Whoever follows me will never walk in darkness, but will have the light of life" (John 8:12). Christians are called to walk in the light, not in darkness.

Not Much of a Man

Darrell Loomis was a truck driver. Each week he hauled goods from Cincinnati to Atlanta. Joe's Diner was his favorite eating spot on the route. Darrell always stopped for meals at Joe's.

One summer afternoon, Darrell parked his truck and walked into the diner. Sitting down in his favorite seat—the third counter stool—he ordered the usual—hot meat loaf sandwich, mashed potatoes, and iced tea. In the distance came a roar and a cloud of dust, followed by the arrival into the parking lot of twelve members of a motorcycle gang, riding Harley-Davidsons with

extended forks. These were fine bikes, quite a sight to see as the gang parked them next to Darrell's Peterbilt truck and set down the kickstands.

As the gang stomped into the diner, the leader immediately spotted Darrell. "Well, who is this little sissy at the counter?" he sneered. Darrell merely remained silent and continued eating his lunch. Forming a semicircle around Darrell, the gang members started snapping their fingers in rhythmic cadence. Unperturbed, Darrell just sat and ate his lunch. One of the gang members picked up Darrell's iced tea and poured it over his head. The others watched, still snapping their fingers in unison. With his napkin Darrell quietly dried his face, but said nothing. Another gang member picked up Darrell's mashed potatoes and stuck a handful into Darrell's ear, wiping his hand on Darrell's back. Darrell remained calm and didn't respond. He simply continued to eat his lunch.

Although the gang continued to harass and taunt Darrell, he never responded to any of it. Even when Darrell finished his lunch, he only stood up, turned to Joe, and silently paid his bill. He left the diner without saying a word.

The leader of the gang laughed and said to Joe, "What a wimp! That guy sure ain't much of a man!"

Joe, looking out the window of the diner said, "No, and he ain't much of a driver either. He just ran over twelve Harleys."

✔ Application:

When Jesus came as the Messiah, He wasn't at all what people expected.

Many looked at Jesus and said, "What a sissy! He sure ain't much of a man! What kind of a Messiah is this?"

Jesus never said a word, though. He took all the abuse that the world could throw at Him. He was ridiculed, humiliated, spat upon, whipped, crowned with thorns, and hung on a cruel cross. Satan did everything he could to destroy Jesus and to make Him the laughingstock of the world. Jesus never opened His mouth. He willingly accepted it because He knew that in the end Satan would be defeated. Satan and all of his demons would ultimately be crushed under the foot of the Savior.

And of course, that's exactly what happened on Calvary.

What a Man!

The Oil Refinery

Once upon a time some visitors took a tour of an oil refinery. The tour guide showed them all the intricacies of the refining process. The vast catalyst chambers, the pipes, the heating vats—everything that went into the refining of oil. As the tour ended, one of the visitors asked the tour guide a simple question. "Sir, you showed us everything except the shipping department. This size oil refinery processes a huge amount of petroleum, turning it into gasoline and lubricants. But you haven't showed us where it's all put into containers and shipped out to the world."

"Well, you see," said the tour guide, "we don't have a shipping department. Everything that is produced in this refinery is used up as energy to keep the refinery going."

✔ Application:

The church has to understand that what it does is for the world, not just to keep itself going. Too many programs that churches run exist for no other purpose than to keep the church going. The purpose of the church is not to sustain itself, but to give what it has away to the world. (See Matthew 28:19 and Mark 16:15.)

Out at Home Plate

The greatest year in baseball history had to be 1924. The World Series that year between the old Washington Senators and the New York Yankees was considered a classic. The series was tied at three games apiece, with the final, seventh game played in Washington.

In the ninth inning of the seventh game, the score was tied, two to two. New York came to bat. Three batters up and three batters down. The Washington fans started screaming. Washington could win the game with a run in the bottom of the ninth.

The first two Washington batters were unable to reach base. With two outs, up to the plate stepped a batter by the name of Gauseland. The fans felt their hopes die because Gauseland was not that good a hitter. The pitcher threw two strikes. Then two balls. When the pitcher threw his fifth pitch, Gauseland stepped into the pitch, and by the crack of the bat you knew the ball was going somewhere way out in left center field.

The center fielder went back. The other fielders also ran toward the fence, hoping the ball would not go over the fence for a home run. The ball hit the top of the fence six inches from the top. It caromed off the fence, and one of the fielders chased it down. Gauseland, meanwhile, was between second and third bases. The third base coach thought this might be the only chance to win, so he waved Gauseland home.

The throw from the outfield was taken first by the shortstop, and then relayed to home plate. Gauseland slid into home just as the catcher pegged him with a perfect throw from the shortstop. Everyone could see that Gauseland had beat the throw. Still, the umpire yelled, "You're OUT!"

The fans went crazy. They threw pop bottles and yelled obscenities when the plate umpire conferred with the other men in black. Then the men on the field signaled for silence. Everybody got quiet. The fans thought they would reverse the call, but the umpire shouted, "The runner is not out because he didn't beat the ball to the plate. He is out because he didn't touch first base!"

It was true. Gauseland was running so hard that he simply failed to touch first. He was out.

✓ Application:

You can do a lot of religious things in your life. You can do a lot of good and noble things, but unless you touch first base, it won't matter too much.

Nicodemus was a good man, but he hadn't touched first base. The rich ruler of Luke 18 was a good man, but he also missed something in his life. To Nicodemus Jesus said, "I tell you the truth, no one can see the kingdom of God unless he is born again" (John 3:3). Jesus doesn't want good people; instead, He wants new people, changed people who have made Him first in their lives.

The Painting of the Last Supper

Leonardo da Vinci painted the fresco "The Last Supper" in a church in Milan. Two very interesting stories are associated with this painting.

Story 1:

 At the time that Leonardo da Vinci painted "The Last Supper," he had an enemy who was a fellow painter. da Vinci had had a bitter argument with this man and despised him. When da Vinci painted the face of Judas Iscariot at the table with Jesus, he used the face of his enemy so that it would be present for ages as the man who betrayed Jesus. He took delight while painting this picture in knowing that others would actually notice the face of his enemy on Judas.

 As he worked on the faces of the other disciples, he often tried to paint the face of Jesus, but couldn't make any progress. da Vinci felt frustrated and confused. In time he realized what was wrong. His hatred for the other painter was holding him back from finishing the face of Jesus. Only after making peace with his fellow painter and repainting the face of Judas was he able to paint the face of Jesus and complete his masterpiece.

☑ Application:

One of the reasons we may have a hard time accepting the forgiveness of God is that we find it hard to forgive others. That's why Jesus said, "If you forgive men when they sin against you, your heavenly Father will also forgive you" (Matt. 6:14, 15). If you want your relationship with Jesus to be all that it should be, forgive your enemies and do all you can to demonstrate Christ's love to them.

Story 2:

One of the reasons the painting took four years to complete was that when da Vinci was almost finished, a friend commented on how incredibly moving the painting was—especially the silver cup on the table. "It was brilliant, beautiful!" he said. "My eyes were immediately drawn to it." da Vinci got so angry that he immediately painted over the cup, blotting it out. The focus of the painting was to be Jesus, not the cup. All attention had to be drawn to Him; anything that detracted from Him had to be removed.

☑ Application:

What is the focus of your life? We need to remove anything that comes before Christ or hinders us from serving him. Christ must be the center of our lives. (See Philippians 1:21.)

Pepe Rodriquez

Pepe Rodriguez, one of the most notorious bank robbers in the early settling of the West, lived just across the border in Mexico. He regularly crept into Texas towns to rob banks, returning to Mexico before the Texas Rangers could catch him.

The frustrated lawmen were so embarrassed by this that they illegally crossed the border into Mexico. Eventually, they cornered Pepe in a Mexican bar that he frequented. Unfortunately, Pepe couldn't speak any English, so the lawmen asked the bartender to translate for them.

The bartender explained to Pepe who these men were, and Pepe began to shake with fear. The Texas Rangers, with their guns drawn, told the bartender to ask Pepe where he had hidden all the money he had stolen from the Texas banks. "Tell him that if he doesn't tell us where the money is right now, we're going to shoot him dead on the spot!"

The bartender translated all this for Pepe. Immediately, Pepe explained in Spanish that the money was hidden in the town well. They could find the money by counting down seventeen stones from the handle, and behind the seventeenth stone was all the loot he had stolen.

The bartender then turned to the Rangers and said in English, "Pepe is a very brave man. He says that you are a bunch of stinking pigs, and he is not afraid to die!"

☑ Application:

Things sometimes get lost in the translation.

Much of what we read and hear and watch is secondhand information that may or may not be true. We need to make sure that we are not only getting the truth, but also communicating the truth to others.

The Prince of Grenada

The prince of Grenada, an heir to the Spanish crown, was sentenced to life in solitary confinement in Madrid's ancient prison called "The Place of the Skull." The fearful, dirty, and dreary nature of the place earned it the name. Everyone knew that once you were in, you would never come out alive. The prince was given one book to read the entire time—the Bible. With only one book to read, he read it over hundreds and hundreds of times. The book became his constant companion.

After thirty-three years of imprisonment, he died. When they came in to clean out his cell, they found some notes he had written using nails to mark the soft stone of the prison walls. The notations were of this sort: Psalm 118:8 is the middle verse of the Bible; Ezra 7:21 contains all the letters of the alphabet except the letter j; the ninth verse of the eighth chapter of Esther is the longest verse in the Bible; no word or name of more than six syllables can be found in the Bible.

When Scot Udell originally noted these facts in an article in *Psychology Today*, he noted the oddity of an individual who spent thirty-three years of his life studying what some have described as the greatest book of all time yet could only glean trivia. From all we know, he never made any religious or spiritual commitment to Christ, but he became an expert at Bible trivia.

✔ Application:

What kind of faith do you have? Is it anything like the faith of the prince of Grenada? There's a difference between knowing facts about God, Jesus Christ, and the Bible, and allowing God to change you from the inside out. Many people grow up knowing a lot about Christianity but never have entrusted their lives to Christ. Have you?

The Queen of England

The queen of England often visits Bob Morrow Castle. On one occasion when she was walking by herself, it started to rain. She rushed to the shelter of the nearest cottage. A lady came to the door who was really ticked off that someone would bother her at that time in the morning. She opened the door a few inches and barked, "What do you want?"

The queen didn't introduce herself. She merely asked, "May I borrow an umbrella?"

"Just a minute," grumbled the woman. She slammed the door, was gone for a moment, and returned bringing the rattiest umbrella she could find, one with broken ribs and small holes. She pushed it through the door and said, "Here." The queen of England thanked her and went on her way with the ragged umbrella.

The next morning, the queen's full escort, dressed in full uniform, pulled up in front of the cottage. One of the escorts knocked on the door and returned the umbrella to the woman saying, "Madam, the Queen of England thanks you." As he walked away he heard her mutter, "If I'd only known, I'd have given her my best."

☑ Application:

Some day we'll all stand before the King of heaven, and some will be heard to mutter, "If I'd only known, I'd have given you my best." The fact is, we do know, and yet many of us still give Christ the scraps, the leftovers, whatever costs us the least.

Because God loved us, He gave us His very best, His Son. (See John 3:16.) Can we give Him anything less than our best?

Real Friends

A teenage boy in Milwaukee, Wisconsin, had cancer and was in the hospital for several weeks to undergo radiation treatments and chemotherapy. During that time, he lost all of his hair. On the way home from the hospital, he was worried—not about the cancer, but about the embarrassment of going back to school with a bald head. He had already decided not to wear a wig or a hat.

When he arrived home, he walked in the front door and turned on the lights. To his surprise, about fifty of his friends jumped up and shouted, "Welcome home!" The boy looked around the room and could hardly believe his eyes—all fifty of his friends had shaved their heads!

☑ Application:

Wouldn't we all like to have caring friends who were so sensitive and committed to us that they would sacrifice their hair for us if that's what it took to make us feel affirmed, included, and loved? Friends like that are hard to find in today's world.

When we become Christians, we are adopted into an extended family of love and support—the church, the body of Christ. The Bible teaches us in I Corinthians 12 that when one member of the body hurts or experiences joy, the whole body shares in that pain or that joy. We suffer together, and we rejoice together. That's what it means to be the church. We are a community, a family—real friends.

When we act this way, we are doing for each other what Jesus Himself did for us. Jesus loved us so much that He did more than shave His head. He went to the cross for us. He gave up His life so that we might live. "Greater love has no one than this, that he lay down his life for his friends" (John 15:13).

The Reverse Thread

"We'll be out until 10:30," said Chad's parents as their friends, the Petersons, came by to pick them up for the banquet. "While we're gone, stay home and finish your history paper."

"Can't I use the car for just a little while?" asked Chad. He had gotten his driver's license just last month. "Um, I need to borrow a book from Todd. I'll only be gone a while."

"Absolutely not," warned Chad's father. "You have all the books you need for tonight. You stay home and work on that paper."

Darn. Chad really wanted to get together with his friends while his parents were gone. After all, his parents weren't using the car, so why shouldn't he be able to? It didn't seem fair. He only wanted to be out for an hour or so. There would still be time to work on his history paper, he reasoned.

The phone rang. It was Todd. "Hey, come on over," he said. "All the guys are here."

Chad decided that he could go to Todd's and get back early enough so that his parents would never know. He just had to be sure to put some gas in the car so nothing would look suspicious. He could work fast on his history paper when he returned.

He got in the car and took off. *No one would ever be the wiser*, he thought. On the way to Todd's, however, disaster struck. He had a flat tire. *Oh great*, he thought. He had never changed a tire before. Now he was going to have to not only change a tire, but also get it repaired quickly so that his parents would never find out. He needed to hurry.

He got out the tire jack and the wrench and went to work. But somehow all of the lug nuts on the wheel were stuck. He couldn't get the tire off. He turned the wrench as hard as he could, but to no avail. After what seemed like hours of trying to get the nuts off, he finally gave up and walked to the nearest gas station. He was exhausted.

It was after ten o'clock when the gas station attendant finally put the hydraulic wrench on the lug nuts and removed the tire. Chad couldn't believe it. *Why couldn't he get those nuts off? Why were they on there so tight? Life wasn't fair!* Now he was going to be put on restriction for the rest of his life!

"Which way were you turning them?" asked the gas station attendant. Chad thought it was a stupid question. Of course he knew how to unscrew a nut. You turn it counterclockwise. "Well," said the attendant, "the threads on this side of the car are reversed. To get them off, you turn them clockwise."

Suddenly Chad felt like a fool.

✓ Application:

A lot of people in the world today have a difficult time finding happiness and fulfillment in life because they are going about it in the wrong way. They are like Chad, turning the nut in the wrong direction—it only gets tighter. Life doesn't get better; it gets worse.

The life that Jesus teaches us to live is like a reverse thread—it's just the opposite of what people think. The world says, "Get all you can!" Jesus says, "Give and it shall be given unto you." The world says, "Only the strong and powerful survive!" Jesus says, "The meek will inherit the earth." The world says, "If someone hurts you, get even!" Jesus says, "Turn the other cheek. Do good to those who treat you badly."

Which way are you turning the wrench? Don't be a fool.

Right Decisions

(This story appears in Ben Patterson's book Waiting *[InterVarsity, 1991].)*

A young man was appointed to the presidency of a bank at the tender age of thirty-two. The promotion was far beyond his wildest dreams and very frightening to him, so he went to the venerable old chairman of the board to ask for advice on how to become a good bank president.

"What is the most important thing for me to do as a new president?" he asked the older man.

"Make right decisions," was the gentleman's terse answer.

The young man thought about that for a moment and said, "Thank you very much; that is very helpful. But can you be a bit more specific? How do I make right decisions?"

The wise old man answered, "Experience."

Exasperated, the young president said, "But sir, that is why I'm here. I don't have the experience I need to make right decisions. How do I get experience?"

"Wrong decisions," came the old man's reply.

✔ Application:

Spiritual maturity doesn't come easily. It usually comes by making a lot of mistakes. Don't get too discouraged if you're unable to live the perfect Christian life right now. That's what commitment is all about. Commitment means that even though you blow it again and again, you hang in there and keep learning from your mistakes. Don't give up on Jesus; He never gives up on you.

Rudolph and Olive

The game show contestant was set to come back the next day for more cash and prizes. All he had to do was correctly answer one last question.

"To be today's champion," the show's smiling host intoned, "name two of Santa's reindeer."

The contestant, a man in his early thirties, gave a sigh of relief, gratified that he had drawn such an easy question.

"Rudolph!" he announced, "and Olive!"

The studio audience started mumbling, and the confused host replied, "Yes, we'll accept Rudolph, but can you explain Olive?"

The man gestured impatiently, "You know, Rudolph—the Red Nosed Reindeer—had a very shiny nose. And if you ever saw it, you would even say it glowed. Olive, the other reindeer. . . ."

☑ Application:

It's amazing how ignorant people are of what Christmas is all about. They can't even get their facts straight about Santa and his reindeer. It's no wonder people don't grasp the importance of the birth of Christ.

The Secret

A pastor and a member of his church made a house call on a rich man. They were seeking donations for another man who had suffered a heart attack. The sick man had no insurance and couldn't afford to pay his medical bills.

The rich man greeted the pastor and his companion warmly and listened as the pastor briefly described the desperate plight of the sick man. "We are asking you for a generous gift," the pastor concluded.

"Who is the sick man?" the host asked.

The pastor shook his head. "Rarely do we reveal the names of people in need. In this case, it's most difficult for the man to admit that he needs charity."

"If I am to be of help, I insist on knowing the identity of the man in need. I will keep it in strictest confidence. I was going to give you $500, but if you tell me the man's name, I will increase the gift to $1,000."

"We will not reveal the man's name," the pastor repeated, shaking his head.

"Two thousand dollars, then. Surely you wouldn't refuse that amount."

"I will not break confidence," the pastor insisted. His companion couldn't believe what he was hearing.

Taking a deep breath, the rich man said, "Three thousand dollars."

Before the pastor could respond, his companion pleaded with him, "Pastor, three thousand dollars will cover almost all of the hospital bills. He is an honorable man. He will keep the secret."

The pastor walked toward the door. "I should have left long ago. The trust and honor of a man are not open to the highest bidder, regardless of the sum of money. I have other visits to make. We will get the money elsewhere."

Before the pastor could leave the house, the rich man begged him to meet together privately in the next room. The moment they were alone he broke into tears. "Reverend, I recently lost every penny I had saved. I am not able to make even a token payment on the mortgage. I have wanted to go to someone for help, but I couldn't stand the idea of everyone in town knowing that I am a failure."

"Now I understand, " the pastor said tenderly. "You were testing me to see if I could be trusted with your secret. I will seek funds for you as well as for the man who is sick. What you have told me will be kept in confidence."

The two men bid their host farewell and headed off to the place of their next visit. "Well, pastor," said the companion, "how much did he give you?"

The pastor smiled and then playfully shook a finger at his friend, "Shame on you. You know such things are a secret."

✓ Application:

How good is your word? Can you be trusted? Most of us are like the pastor's friend. We find it hard to believe that someone would keep his word—especially when large sums of money are involved. After all, the end justifies the means, right?

God can be trusted with every thought, every desire, every problem we face, every doubt we have, every sin we commit. He can be trusted to listen to us and to keep His word to us. When He says He will forgive and forget, we can put that in the bank. Our sins are gone, forever. God doesn't hold grudges. He won't betray us. God is absolutely reliable and trustworthy.

Sharpen Your Axe

Some years ago a young man looking for work approached a foreman of a logging crew and asked him for a job. "It depends," replied the foreman. "Let's see you take this one down."

The young man stepped forward and skillfully felled a great tree. The foreman was impressed and exclaimed, "You can start on Monday!"

Monday, Tuesday, and Wednesday rolled by. Thursday afternoon the foreman approached the young man and said, "You can pick up your paycheck on the way out today."

Startled, the young man asked, "I thought you paid on Fridays."

"Normally we do," answered the foreman, "but we're letting you go today because you've fallen behind. Our daily charts show that you've dropped from first place on Monday to last place on Wednesday."

"But I'm a hard worker," the young man objected. "I arrive first, leave last, and I've even worked through my coffee breaks!"

The foreman, sensing the boy's integrity, thought for a minute and then asked, "Have you been sharpening your ax?"

The young man replied, "Well, no, sir. I've been working too hard to take the time."

☑ Application:

How about you? Too busy to sharpen your ax? Prayer is the hone that gives you the sharp edge. Without prayer, the more work you do, the duller you'll get. We need to take time to stay sharp as we go about the work of Christ's kingdom!

The Smartest Teenager in the World

One fine day four people were flying in a small, four-passenger plane: a pilot, a minister, and two teenagers, one of whom had just won an award for being the "Smartest Teenager in the World."

As they were flying along, the pilot turned to the three passengers and said, "I've got some bad news, and I've got some worse news. The bad news is, we're out of gas. The plane's going down and we're gonna crash. The worse news is, I only have three parachutes on board."

This meant, of course, that someone would have to go down with the plane.

The pilot continued. "I have a wife and three children at home. I have many responsibilities. I'm sorry, but I'm going to have to take one of the parachutes." With that, he grabbed one of the chutes and jumped out of the plane.

The Smartest Teenager in the World was next to speak. "I'm the Smartest Teenager in the World," he said. "I might be the one who comes up with a cure for cancer or AIDS or solves the world's economic problems. Everyone is counting on me!" The Smartest Teenager in the World grabbed the second parachute and jumped.

The minister then spoke up and said, "Son, you take the last parachute. I've made my peace with God, and I'm willing to go down with the plane. Now take the last parachute and go."

"Relax, reverend," said the other teenager. "The Smartest Teenager in the World just jumped out of the plane with my knapsack."

✔ Application:

A lot of kids think they're pretty smart. In reality, they're a lot like The Smartest Teenager in the World. They jump out into the world without parachutes. They think they know it all and have all they need to live happy and fulfilled lives, to keep them from crashing and burning. What they actually have is a knapsack. The only parachute that will ultimately save is the Gospel of Christ. All other ways are false and lead to death. Jesus said, "I am the way and the truth and the life. No one comes to the Father except through me" (John 14:6).

A lot of smart kids haven't learned how to make wise decisions. They act impulsively, without thinking. The result is sometimes the same as what happened to the Smartest Teenager in the World—death.

The Society Woman

A good-looking society woman was invited to an expensive fund-raising dinner in New York City. She was seated next to a wealthy lawyer. During the meal, they had a chance to get to know each other and were having a good time. When the meal was finished, the lawyer leaned over and asked the woman if she would go to bed with him for $10,000. The woman blushed but said that she would. The man then asked her if she would go to bed with him for $10. The woman was shocked and said, "What kind of a woman do you think I am?" The man responded, "My dear, we have already established that. Now we are merely deciding on the price."

Application:

What's your price? What would it take to cause you to sell out? We already know who we are. We are sinners who have been saved by faith in Christ. None of us is immune to sinful behavior. Even Paul the apostle stumbled and fell. Peter, when faced with possible persecution at the time of the Crucifixion, denied Christ three times. He had his price.

Both Peter and Paul grew in their faith, though, becoming strong and courageous. Both of them died as martyrs because no amount of money, no amount of pain could cause them to turn their backs on their Lord.

Some of us are fair-weather Christians. We stick with Christ until something better comes up, or until the going gets rough. Our goal as Christians is to allow Christ, through the power of the Holy Spirit, to make us into the kind of people who are strong, firm, and steadfast in faith. (See I Peter 5:10.)

Sparky, the Loser

Once upon a time, there was a little boy the other children called "Sparky," after a comic strip horse named Sparkplug. Even though the boy hated that nickname, he could never shake it.

School was difficult for Sparky. He failed every subject in the eighth grade. He flunked physics in high school. In fact, he still holds the school record for being the worst physics student in the school's history. He also flunked Latin, algebra, and English. He didn't do much better in sports. He made the school's golf team, but his poor play ended up costing his team the championship.

Throughout his youth, Sparky was a loser socially. Not that he was actively disliked by other kids—it's just that nobody paid much attention to him. He was astonished if a classmate even said hello outside of school. He never dated or even asked a girl out. He was afraid of being turned down. Sparky didn't let being a loser bother him that much; he just decided to make it through life the best he could and not worry about what other people thought of him.

Sparky did, however, have a hobby. He loved cartoons, and he liked drawing his own cartoons. No one else thought they were any good, however. When he was a senior in high school, he submitted some cartoons to the school yearbook and they were rejected. Sparky kept drawing anyway.

Sparky dreamed about being an artist for Walt Disney. After graduating from high school, he wrote a letter to Walt Disney Studios inquiring about job opportunities. He received a form letter requesting samples of his artwork. The form letter asked him to draw a funny cartoon of "a man repairing a clock by shoveling the springs and gears back inside it."

Sparky drew the cartoon and mailed it off with some of his other work to Disney studios. He waited and waited for a reply. Finally the reply came—another form letter telling him that there was no job for him.

Sparky was disappointed but not surprised. He had always been a loser, and this was just one more loss. In a weird way, he thought, his life was kind of funny. He tried telling his own life story in cartoons—a childhood full of the misadventures of a little boy loser, a chronic underachiever. This cartoon character has now become known by the whole world. The boy who failed the eighth grade, the young artist whose work was rejected not only by Walt Disney Studios but by his own high school yearbook, was Charles Monroe "Sparky" Schultz—creator of the "Peanuts" comic strip and the little boy loser whose kite never flies: Charlie Brown.

✓ Application:

We have all experienced rejection and failure in life, but God has gifted each one of us with unique talents and abilities that enable us to make a significant contribution to the world. What are your gifts? Unless you attempt to use them, you will never discover how God prepared you to contribute. We need to be like the little boy in Scripture who offered Jesus his lunch—Jesus in turn used it to feed a multitude. (See John 6:9.)

The Suicide Attempt

A few years ago a woman was standing on top of a fifty-four-story building in New York City, ready to jump to her death. The police suicide squad took her threats extremely seriously. She didn't look the type, in her expensive dress and with her distinguished appearance, but regardless of her appearance, every attempt to convince her to get down from the ledge ended in failure.

One of the police officers called his pastor to come to the scene and pray for the woman. His pastor came, and after appraising the situation, asked the police captain if he might try to get close enough to talk with the woman. The captain shrugged and said, "Sure, what have we got to lose?"

The pastor started walking toward the woman, but she screamed as before, "Don't come any closer or I'll jump!" He took a step backward and called out to her, "I'm sorry that you believe no one loves you."

This got her attention and also the attention of the suicide squad—it was such an unusual thing to say. "Your children and grandchildren must not love you. Apparently they never give you any attention," he continued.

With this, the woman took a step toward the pastor and said, "My grandchildren do love me. My whole family does. My grandchildren are wonderful. I have eight grandchildren."

The pastor took a step toward the woman and said, "Well then, you must be very poor, or you wouldn't want to take your own life."

The woman, who was obviously overweight, said, "Do I look like I go without meals? We live in a very nice apartment in Central Park. I'm not poor!"

The pastor then took another step and was now only three feet from her. "Then why do you want to kill yourself? I don't understand."

The woman thought for a moment and said, "You know, I don't really remember."

☑ Application:

This true story ended with the pastor escorting the woman off the ledge while she showed him pictures of her grandchildren. She eventually became a volunteer on the city's suicide hotline, helping others to choose life. The pastor helped her get her eyes off herself and onto the many ways that God had blessed her. She learned that thankful people are happy people. "Give thanks to the God of heaven. His love endures forever" (Ps. 136:26).

Teddy and Miss Thompson

Miss Thompson was a schoolteacher who every year would say to her students, "Boys and girls, I love you all the same. I have no favorites." Of course, she wasn't being completely truthful. Teachers do have favorites and, what's worse, most teachers have students that they simply don't like.

Teddy Stallard was a boy that Miss Thompson simply didn't like, and for good reason. He didn't seem interested in school. He wore a deadpan, blank expression on his face, and his eyes were glassy and unfocused. When she spoke to Teddy, he merely shrugged his shoulders. His clothes were mussed and his hair unkempt. He wasn't an attractive boy, and he certainly wasn't likable.

Whenever she marked Teddy's papers, she got a certain perverse pleasure out of putting X's next to the wrong answers. When she put the F's at the top of the papers, she did it with a flair. She should have known better; she had Teddy's records, and she knew more about him than she wanted to admit. The records read:

1st Grade: Teddy shows promise with his work and attitude, but poor home situation.

2nd Grade: Teddy could do better. Mother is seriously ill. He receives little help at home.

3rd Grade: Teddy is a good boy, but too serious. He is a slow learner. His mother died this year.

4th Grade: Teddy is very slow, but well-behaved. His father shows no interest.

At Christmas, the boys and girls in Miss Thompson's class brought her presents, piled them on her desk, and crowded around to watch her open them. Among the presents was one from Teddy Stallard. She was surprised that he had brought her a gift. Teddy's gift was wrapped in brown paper and held together with Scotch tape. On the paper were written the simple words, "For Miss Thompson. From Teddy." When she opened Teddy's present, out fell a gaudy rhinestone bracelet, with half the stones missing, and a bottle of cheap perfume.

The other boys and girls began to giggle and smirk over Teddy's gifts, but Miss Thompson at least had enough sense to silence them by immediately putting on the bracelet and dotting some of the perfume on her wrist. Holding her wrist up for the other children to smell, she said, "Doesn't it smell lovely?" The other children, taking their cue from the teacher, readily agreed with "oohs" and "ahs."

When school was over and the other children had left, Teddy lingered behind. He slowly came over to her desk and said softly, "Miss Thompson?

Miss Thompson, you smell just like my mother . . . and her bracelet looks real pretty on you too. I'm glad you liked my presents."

When Teddy left, Miss Thompson got down on her knees and asked God to forgive her.

The next day when the children came to school, they were welcomed by a new teacher. Miss Thompson had become a different person. She was no longer just a teacher; she had become an agent of God, committed to loving her children and doing things for them that would live on after her. She helped all the children, but especially the slow ones, and especially Teddy Stallard. By the end of that school year, Teddy showed dramatic improvement. He caught up with most of the students and was even ahead of some.

Once the school year ended, Miss Thompson didn't hear from Teddy for a long time. Then one day she received a note that read:

Dear Miss Thompson,

I wanted you to be the first to know. I will be graduating second in my class.

Love, Teddy Stallard

Four years later, another note came:

Dear Miss Thompson,

They just told me I will be graduating first in my class. I wanted you to be the first to know. The university has not been easy, but I have had a good four years.

Love, Teddy Stallard

And, four years later:

Dear Miss Thompson,

As of today, I am Theodore Stallard, M.D. How about that? I wanted you to be the first to know. I am getting married next month, the twenty-seventh to be exact. I want you to come and sit where my mother would sit if she were alive. You are the only family I have now. Dad died last year.

Love, Teddy Stallard

Miss Thompson went to that wedding and sat where Teddy's mother would have sat. She deserved to be there; she had done something for Teddy that he could never forget.

☑ Application:

We can also become agents of God as we reach out to help those who are rejected by others, or those who have great needs that we become aware of. That is what Christ in Matthew 25:31-46 teaches us that we should do. Whenever we help someone like Teddy, we are helping Jesus Himself.

Miss Thompson was a lot like Barnabas, who was an encourager. (See Acts 11:23, 24.) Many people around us need someone to believe in them and build them up rather than tear them down. When we see someone who is different from us or handicapped or lonely, we can tease them and put them down—or we can do what Barnabas and Jesus would do: show kindness, love, and encouragement.

Telemachus Goes to Rome

Saint Telemachus, a fourth-century monk who lived in a monastery, felt God calling him to Rome. He couldn't figure out why God would want him in Rome, but he felt the pressure to go. Putting his possessions in a little satchel, he threw the bag over his shoulder and started out over the dusty, westward roads to Rome.

When he got to Rome, people were running about the city in great confusion. He had arrived on a day when the gladiators were going to fight both other gladiators and animals in the amphitheater. Everyone was heading to the amphitheater to watch the entertainment.

Telemachus thought this must be why God had called him to Rome. He walked into the amphitheater. He sat down among 80,000 people who cheered as the gladiators came out proclaiming, "Hail Caesar! We die to the glory of Caesar."

The little monk thought to himself, *Here we are, four centuries after Christ, in a civilized nation, and people are killing one another for the entertainment of the crowd. This isn't Christian!*

Telemachus got up out of his seat, ran down the steps, climbed over the wall, walked out to the center of the amphitheater, and stood between two large gladiators. Putting his hands up, he meekly cried out, "In the name of Christ, stop!" The crowd laughed and jeered. One of the gladiators slapped Telemachus in the stomach with his sword and sent him spinning off into the dust.

Telemachus got up and again stood between the two huge gladiators. He repeated, "In the name of Christ, stop." This time the crowd chanted "Run him through!" One of the gladiators took his sword and ran it through Telemachus's stomach. He fell into the dust and the sand turned red as blood ran out of him. One last time, Telemachus weakly cried out, "In the name of Christ, stop." He died on the amphitheater floor.

The crowd grew silent, and within minutes they emptied out of the amphitheater. History records that, thanks to Saint Telemachus, this was the last gladiatorial contest in the history of the Roman Empire.

Saint Telemachus changed the course of history. So can you. God loves to use one person to make a big difference in the world—and God wants to use you.

The best example we have is when God sent His Son, Jesus, to die on the cross for our sins. One man made the greatest difference in the history of the world. God still works through individuals to accomplish His will. Will you be the one He uses next?

Thermometers and Thermostats

(This illustration could be an object lesson if you bring in a thermometer and a thermostat for students to see.)

Do you know the difference between a thermostat and a thermometer?

A thermometer merely tells what the temperature is in a particular area. If your thermometer reads seventy degrees and you place that thermometer in a room that is currently eighty degrees, the thermometer will change to register whatever the room temperature is. It won't be long before the thermometer reads eighty degrees. It always adjusts to its environment.

The thermostat, however, adjusts the room temperature. If the thermostat is set at seventy degrees and the room is eighty degrees, the temperature of the room changes to conform to whatever the thermostat is reading. The room will become seventy degrees.

☑ Application:

You live your life as either a thermostat or a thermometer. You can either blend in with the crowd, or you can change the crowd. You are either influencing others, or they are influencing you.

Jesus calls us to become thermostats. Actually, since they didn't have thermostats in Bible times, Jesus used the terms "salt" and "light" to communicate that we are to be agents of change in the world. (See Matthew 5:13-16.)

Thomas Edison, the Failure

Biographers have written that Thomas Edison, the inventor of the light bulb, made over nine hundred light bulbs that didn't work before he finally made one that did. Nine hundred times he went to all the trouble of making a light bulb, plugging it in, flipping the switch, and watching while nothing happened. People must have thought he was nuts, but he kept on trying. According to Edison, every time he made a light bulb that didn't work, he merely found "one more way not to make a light bulb." Eventually, by the process of elimination, he made a light bulb that produced light. As a result, he is known as one of the greatest inventors of all time.

☑ Application:

Most of us don't realize how many failures successful people endure before they achieve their purposes. We only hear about the one time they succeed. What made Edison great was his commitment to making a light bulb. He didn't let his failures discourage him. He hung in there and kept trying, even though he kept goofing up.

So it is with the Christian life. Most Christians we look up to failed many times before arriving where they are today. The apostle Paul admitted as much in Romans 7. "I mess up all the time!" he moaned. "The things I want to do, I don't do, and vice versa." But Paul kept on running the race, striving to reach his goal, the finish line. (See Philippians 3:14.) He never gave up. That's commitment. Being committed doesn't mean you are successful all the time. It means you hang in there. You keep on making mistakes. Like Edison, you learn from your mistakes one more way *not* to live the Christian life.

The Three Spinners

Introduce this old tale from Grimm's *Fairy Tales* by explaining that spinning was the term used for using a spinning wheel to make yarn out of flax.

There was once a girl who was lazy and would not spin. Her mother could not persuade her to do it, no matter how hard she tried. Finally the mother became so angry that she gave her daughter a good beating. While the mother was beating the girl, the queen of the realm happened to pass by and heard the girl crying. The queen stopped, entered the house, and asked the mother why she was beating her child.

The woman was ashamed to tell of her daughter's laziness, so she said, "I am trying to stop her from spinning. That's all she wants to do. Day and night, she keeps on spinning, but I am poor and cannot supply her with enough flax."

The queen answered, "I like nothing better than the sound of the spinning wheel, and I always feel happy when I hear its humming. Let me take your daughter with me to the castle. I have plenty of flax, and she shall spin there to her heart's content."

The mother was only too glad to get rid of her daughter, so she agreed to let the queen take the girl with her. When they reached the castle, the queen showed her three rooms completely filled with the finest flax in the land.

"Now you can spin all of this flax," said the queen "and if you are able to spin it all to my satisfaction, I will make you the wife of my eldest son. You will become the princess. But if you fail, you will be banished from the realm forever."

Even though the girl was momentarily excited about the possibility of becoming the princess, she was inwardly terrified because she knew couldn't spin the flax even if she were to live a hundred years and were to sit spinning every day of her life from morning to evening. She didn't even know how. For three days she sat and cried, without spinning a single thread. On the third day the queen came, and when she saw that nothing had been done, she was surprised and asked for an explanation. The girl excused herself by saying that she had not been able to begin because of the distress she felt from leaving home and her loving mother. The excuse satisfied the queen temporarily, but as she left she said, "Tomorrow you must begin to work."

When the girl was alone again, she couldn't figure out what to do at all. In her frustration, she gazed out the window and saw three women who were passing by. One had a broad flat foot that caused her to walk with a limp, the second had a fat lower lip that hung down under her chin, and the third had a huge thumb that looked ugly and sore. When they saw the girl, they stopped at the window and asked what the girl was doing. The girl told them her plight, and the three women said, "We are spinners, and we will help you on one condition. When you marry the prince, invite us to your wedding, and do not be ashamed of us. Call us your cousins, and let us sit at your table. If you will promise this, we will finish off your flax-spinning in a very short time."

"Oh yes, I promise with all my heart," the girl answered. "Only come in now and begin at once."

The women came in and began spinning the yarn immediately. The first one drew out the thread and pumped the treadle that turned the wheel; the second moistened the thread with her mouth, and the third twisted it with her thumb. Soon heaps of beautiful yarn began falling to the ground. Whenever the queen came by, the girl would hide the three spinsters and keep them out of sight. The queen was amazed at the heaps of well-spun yarn, and there was no end to the praise that the girl received. When the first room was empty, they went on to the second, and then to the third, so that at last all the flax was spun.

Then the three women left, saying to the girl, "Do not forget your promise, and nothing bad will happen to you."

When the girl showed the delighted queen the three empty rooms and the heaps of beautiful yarn, the wedding was arranged at once. The prince was quite pleased that he was to have such a diligent and hard-working wife.

"I have three cousins," said the girl, "and they have been very kind to me over the years. May I invite them to the wedding, and ask them to sit at the head table with us?"

The queen and the prince both said, "Yes, that would be permitted."

When the wedding feast began, in came the three spinsters and sat down at the head table. The prince was surprised at their appearance. "Oh," he said, "I didn't realize that you had such dreadfully ugly relatives."

He went up to the first spinster and looking down at her broad, flat foot, asked, "How did your foot become so large?"

"From pumping the treadle on the spinning wheel," she said. "From pumping."

He then went up to the second spinster and said, "How is it that you have such a great hanging lip?"

"From licking the thread," she answered. "From licking."

Then he asked the third, "How is it that you have such a huge thumb?"

"From twisting the thread," she replied. "From twisting."

The prince considered all this for moment and then announced, "From this day forward, my beautiful bride will never again touch a spinning wheel!"

And together they lived happily ever after.

☑ Application:

As you were listening to this story, did you keep thinking, *Uh oh. Pretty soon she's going to be found out! She's going to be in deep trouble.*

That's not the way the story turns out. Even though the girl is lazy, deceptive, and unworthy of being made a princess, she gets away with it. Nothing bad happens to her, and she's off the hook forever. The story has a wonderfully happy ending.

That's the story of the Gospel. That's what grace is all about. Like the girl, you and I are lazy, dishonest, and undeserving of anything except banishment from the realm. But God in His great mercy sent His Son so that we would never ever have to pay the penalty for our sin. Just as the three spinsters carried the burden of spinning for the girl, Jesus bore our sins on the cross and we are set free. God has given us His kingdom. We are adopted into His forever family. It's like a fairy tale—the only difference is, it's true!

The Tightrope and the Wheelbarrow

The story is told of a great circus performer by the name of Blondin who stretched a long steel cable across Niagara Falls. During high winds and without a safety net, he walked, ran, and even danced across the tightrope to the amazement and delight of the large crowd of people who watched.

Once he took a wheelbarrow full of bricks and amazed the crowd by pushing it effortlessly across the cable, from one side of the falls to the other. Blondin then turned to the crowd and asked, "Now, how many of you believe that I could push a man across the wire in the wheelbarrow?"

The vote was unanimous. Everyone cheered and held their hands high.

They all believed he could do it!

"Then," asked Blondin, "would one of you please volunteer to be that man?"

As quickly as the hands went up, they went back down. Not a single person would volunteer to ride in the wheelbarrow and to trust his life to Blondin.

☑ Application:

Many people say to Jesus, "Yes, I believe!" If you are among those who say that, are you willing to demonstrate your belief by trusting your life to Him? Are you willing to get in the wheelbarrow and to risk everything on your faith? That's what it means to believe. Faith is not just an intellectual exercise. It involves total commitment.

Too Many Engineers

One of the worst train disasters in history occurred in the El Toro Tunnel in Leon, Spain, on January 3, 1944. Over five hundred people died.

The train was one of those long passenger trains with an engine on both ends. On this particular day, when the train went into the El Toro Tunnel, the engine on the front stalled. When the front engine stopped, the engineer on the back engine started up his engine to back the train out of the tunnel. At the same time, however, the front engineer managed to get the front engine started again and attempted to continue the journey. Neither engineer had any way of communicating with the other. Both engineers thought they simply needed more power. They continued to pull in both directions for several minutes. Hundreds of passengers on the train in the tunnel died of carbon monoxide poisoning because the train could not make up its mind which way to go.

☑ Application:

The people on that train died because the train had one too many engineers. Many of us struggle as to which way to go with our lives—whether to come to Jesus or to remain in our sin. This indecision can cause us to miss out on the most important decision in our lives. Sometimes we think we can have it both ways, but we can't. We can't serve God and also serve the devil. Jesus Himself warned us against trying to live a double life: "No one can serve two masters" (Matt. 6:24a).

The Tractor Pull

Tractor pulls are increasing in popularity, thanks to television coverage of many live events around the country. For the uninitiated, the "tractor" in these events is really more like a rocket with four wheels. Some of these tractors have multiple engines and are longer than a truck. The tractor-like rear wheels are about the only item on the machine that resemble an ordinary farm tractor.

These high-powered tractors are hitched to a wedge-shaped trailer that creates greater resistance the farther it is pulled. The tractor, racing toward the finish line, usually starts out strong in pulling the trailer, but quickly labors and often stalls under the ever-increasing resistance. The wheels of the tractor often spin so rapidly that the tractor becomes literally stuck in the mud, spinning its wheels and unable to continue. Only when the trailer is unhitched from the tractor can the tractor move again—and then perhaps only with assistance.

☑ Application:

Sin is the trailer in our lives. The effects of sin may be slight at first, but the longer we carry it and struggle with it, the more difficult it becomes. The weight of sin eventually causes us to stall. Only God can "unhitch" the sin from our lives, through the sacrifice of Jesus Christ. Even Christians can labor from pulling a "sin-trailer," eventually becoming bogged down in the effects of sin. Not until that sin is released and Christ assists an individual to begin again can the Christian continue the race unhindered. "But thanks be to God! He gives us the victory through our Lord Jesus Christ" (I Cor. 15:57).

The Turtle Picnic

A turtle family went on a picnic. They had prepared seven years for their outing. The family left home, searching for a suitable place. During the second year of their journey, they found it. For about six months they cleared the area, unpacked the picnic basket, and completed the arrangements. They discovered, however, that they had forgotten the salt. A picnic without salt would be a disaster, they all agreed.

After a lengthy discussion, the youngest turtle was chosen to retrieve the salt at home. Although he was the fastest of the slow-moving turtles, the little turtle whined, cried, and wobbled in his shell. He agreed to go on only one condition: that no one would eat until he returned. The family consented and the little turtle left.

Three years passed—and the little turtle had not returned. Five years. Six years. Then in the seventh year of his absence, the eldest turtle could no longer contain his hunger. He announced that he was going to eat and began

to unwrap a sandwich. At that point, the little turtle suddenly popped out from behind a tree shouting, "SEE! I knew you wouldn't wait! Now, I'm not going to get the salt."

Some of us, like that little turtle, don't trust anyone or give anyone the benefit of the doubt. We waste away our whole lives waiting for people to live up to our poor expectations of them—and they always do.

We can be thankful that God doesn't treat us that way. He accepts us just the way we are. He believes in us. He cheers us on. He thinks the best of us. He is proud of us. When we mess up, He forgives and forgets, and gives us another opportunity to do good. That's how God treats us, and that's how we are to treat others. Let's not think the worst of each other. Let's expect the best.

Uncompromising Determination

A farmer was driving down the road one day and noticed a sign by the local airport that said "EXPERIENCE THE THRILL OF FLYING." The farmer thought to himself, *Tomorrow is my wife's birthday. I'd love for her to experience the thrill of flying. That would sure make a nice birthday present.*

The farmer went into the airport and after some time found a pilot who would take him and his wife on a flight over their farm. The pilot owned a small open-cockpit plane that would certainly give his wife a thrill, but the pilot's price was too high. The farmer bartered with the pilot for a long time, insisting on a lower price. Finally, the pilot agreed to the lower price, on one condition: the farmer and his wife had to promise not to say a single word during the entire flight. One word spoken aloud, however small, would increase the price to the pilot's original fee. The farmer's determination to give his wife the thrill of flying was only surpassed by his determination to spend as little money as possible, so he agreed to the condition.

The next morning the three of them took off and soon were high in the air. The pilot knew that if he did a few roller-coaster dips and turns with the plane, the couple in the backseat would soon speak up and he would receive the higher price. With that in mind, the pilot dipped and turned, climbed and dived, even did a few loop-de-loops. But not a sound was uttered. Not a scream, not a whimper. Nothing but silence.

As they were landing, the pilot, amazed at the determination of his passengers, yelled back to the farmer, "I can't believe you didn't say something up there! Why, I dipped and turned, climbed and dived as never before, but you two were quiet the whole time. I guess you win!"

The old farmer shouted back, "Well, you almost won, son. You almost won. I sure felt like hollerin' when my wife fell out."

✔ Application:

That old farmer was determined to get what he wanted on his terms. He got it, but with a result that he probably hadn't counted on. Some of us are like that. We can be amazingly determined to have things our way. We let pride and stubbornness get in the way of listening to reason or doing what we know is right.

Are you like that sometimes? You know what God wants, but you want something else. Before long there is a battle of the wills. Who is going to win? The truth is, you may win a battle or two, but you will always lose the war. If you are a strong-willed person, with a mind of your own, God wants you! God wants to transform and to channel your determination into a determination to serve Christ and to stick with Him no matter what. God is looking for people who stubbornly refuse to turn away from Jesus Christ.

The W.C.

In the days when you couldn't count on a public facility to have indoor plumbing, a English woman was planning a trip to Germany. She was registered to stay in a small zimmer, a guest house owned by the local schoolmaster and his wife. The traveler was concerned, however, about whether or not the guest house contained a W.C. (In England a bathroom is commonly referred to as the "W.C.", which stands for "water closet.") She wrote the schoolmaster a letter, inquiring into the location of the W.C. The schoolmaster, not a fluent speaker of English, asked the local parish priest if he knew the meaning of "W.C." Together they pondered possible meanings of the letters and finally decided they must be referring to a wayside chapel. Apparently, they concluded, the lady wanted to know if there was a wayside chapel somewhere near the house. The schoolmaster wrote the following reply to the English lady:

My Dear Madam:

I take great pleasure in informing you that the W.C. is situated nine miles from the house in the center of a beautiful grove of pine trees surrounded by lovely grounds.

It is capable of holding 229 people, and it is open on Sundays and Thursdays only. As there are a great number of people expected during the summer months, I suggest that you come early, although usually there is plenty of standing room. This is an unfortunate situation, especially if you are in the habit of going regularly. It may be of some interest to you to know that my daughter was married in the W.C. and it was there that she met her husband. I can remember the rush there was for seats. Why there were ten people to every seat usually occupied by one. It was wonderful to see the expressions on their faces.

You will be glad to hear that a good number of people bring their lunch and make a day of it, while others wait until the last minute and arrive just on time. I would especially recommend your ladyship to go on Thursdays when there is an organ accompaniment. The acoustics are excellent, and even the most delicate sounds can be heard everywhere.

The newest addition is a bell, which rings every time a person enters. A bazaar is to be held to provide plush seats for all, since the people feel it is long needed. My wife has been ill, and so she hasn't been able to go recently. It has been almost a year since she went last, which naturally pains her very much.

I shall be delighted to reserve the best seat for you, where you shall be seen by all. In fact, I look forward to escorting you there myself.

With kindest regards,

The Schoolmaster

☑ Application:

The schoolmaster's letter is a good example of miscommunication. When we communicate with others, we need to be careful that we know what we're talking about, and that people hear what we are saying.

We'll Get Back to You

Dear Christians:

This is My commission to you—in fact, you might even call it a great commission. You are to go to all people everywhere and call them to become My disciples. You are to baptize them and teach them to obey all that I have commanded you.

Don't forget. I will be with you always to help you, even to the end of the world. I will never leave you nor forsake you, because I love you. Please don't forsake Me.

With all My love,
Jesus Christ

Dear Jesus Christ:

We acknowledge the receipt of Your recent communication.

Your proposal is both interesting and challenging; however, due to a shortage of personnel, as well as several other financial and personal considerations, we do not feel that we can give proper emphasis to Your challenge at this time.

A committee has been appointed to study the feasibility of the plan. We should have a report to bring to our congregation sometime in the future. You may rest assured that we will give this our careful consideration, and our board will be praying for You and Your efforts to find additional disciples.

We do appreciate Your offer to serve as a resource person, and should we decide to undertake this project at some point in the future, we'll get back to You.

Cordially,
The Christians

☑ Application:

How have you responded to Christ's commission to go and make disciples? (See Matthew 28:19, 20.)

What Life?

He saw people love each other, and he saw that love made strenuous demands on the lovers. He saw that love required sacrifice and self-denial. He saw that love produced arguments, jealousy, and sorrow. He decided that love cost too much. He decided not to diminish his life with love.

He saw people strive for distant and hazy goals. He saw men strive for success and women strive for high ideals. He saw that the striving was often mixed with disappointment. He saw strong and committed men fail, and he saw weak, undeserving men succeed. He saw that striving sometimes forced people into pettiness and greed. He decided that it cost too much. He decided not to soil his life with striving.

He saw people serving others. He saw men give money to the poor and helpless. He saw that the more they served, the faster the need grew. He saw ungrateful receivers turn on their serving friends. He decided not to soil his life with serving.

When he died, he walked up to God and presented his life to Him—undiminished, unmarred, unsoiled. The man was clean and untouched by the filth of the world, and he presented himself to God proudly saying, "Here is my life!"

And God said, "Life? What life?"

☑ Application:

God doesn't want us to insulate ourselves from the pain and suffering of the world. When we love others, serve others, and strive to be all that God wants us to be, we get dirty, we get hurt, we get used. But those are the battle scars that God wants to see when we face Him someday. God wants us to get in the game and get our uniforms dirty. That's what Jesus did when He came into the world. He didn't choose to play it safe; neither should we. "To this you were called, because Christ suffered for you, leaving you an example, that you should follow in his steps" (I Peter. 2:21).

When Do I Die?

A family was involved in a serious traffic accident. Mike, the youngest of two brothers involved, was badly injured and needed a blood transfusion. Mike's big brother Danny, who was only eight years old, had the same blood type as his younger brother. The dad sat down with Danny and carefully explained to him why this blood transfusion was needed and how wonderful it would be for his little brother. After some silence, Danny responded by saying, "Yes, Daddy, I'll give my blood to Mike so he can get well."

At the hospital, a pint of blood was drawn from Danny's veins. Only after the needle was removed did Danny turn to his father with tears rolling down his cheeks and ask, "Daddy, when do I die?"

The father suddenly realized with a shock that Danny had misunderstood his explanation of giving blood. Danny thought he was giving all of his blood to save the life of his brother! He thought that he would die after the transfusion was over. Yet he still had agreed to help his little brother.

☑ Application:

Danny was willing to die so that his little brother would live. That's what Christ did for each of us. He shed His own blood to give us life. "He died for us so that . . . we may live together with him" (I Thess. 5:10).

The Window

Mr. Wilson and Mr. Thayer, both seriously ill, shared a small room in a hospital. The room was just large enough for the pair of them—two beds, two bedside lockers, a door opening on the hall, and one window looking out on the world.

Mr. Wilson, as part of his treatment, was allowed to sit up in bed for an hour in the afternoon (something to do with draining fluid from his lungs). His bed was next to the window. Mr. Thayer, however, had to spend all his time flat on his back. Both of them had to remain quiet and still, which was the reason they were in the small room by themselves. They were grateful for the peace and privacy, though. None of the bustle and clatter and prying eyes of the general ward for them. Of course, one of the disadvantages of their condition was that they weren't allowed to do much. No reading, no radio, certainly no television. They had to pass their days quiet and still, just the two of them.

They passed the long morning hours talking about their wives, their children, their homes, their jobs, their hobbies, what they did during the war, where they'd been on vacations. Every afternoon, however, when Mr. Wilson was propped up for his hour, he would pass the time by describing what he saw happening through the window beside his bed. Mr. Thayer began to live for that hour.

The window apparently overlooked a park with a lake where there were ducks and swans, children throwing them bread and sailing model boats, and young lovers walking hand in hand beneath the trees. There were flowers and stretches of grass, games of softball, people relaxing in the sunshine, and right at the back, behind the fringe of trees, there was a fine view of the city skyline. Mr. Thayer would listen to all of this, enjoying every minute of it—a child nearly fell into the lake, beautiful girls in their summer dresses strolled in the park, a ball game came to an exciting conclusion, a boy played with his puppy. It got to the place that he could almost see what was happening outside.

One fine afternoon when there was a parade passing by, Mr. Thayer thought, *Why should Wilson get to be next to the window and have all the pleasure of seeing what was going on? Why shouldn't I have the chance too?* He felt ashamed for thinking like that, but the more he tried to put the thought out of his mind, the more strongly he wanted to be the one to see all those sights. He would do anything, he felt, for a chance to be by the window. Within a few days Mr. Thayer had turned completely sour. He should be by the window. He lost sleep brooding about it and grew even more seriously ill, which the doctors

couldn't understand.

One night as Mr. Thayer stared at the ceiling, Mr. Wilson suddenly awoke, coughing and choking, the fluid congesting in his lungs. His hands groped for the call button that would bring the night nurse running. Mr. Thayer didn't move. The coughing racked on and on in the darkness. Mr. Wilson choked one final time, and then stopped breathing altogether. Mr. Thayer continued to stare at the ceiling.

In the morning, when the day nurse came into the room with water for their baths, she found Mr. Wilson dead. With no fuss, his body was quietly taken away.

As soon as it seemed decent, Mr. Thayer asked if he could be moved to the bed next to the window. The doctor agreed to let him be moved, and the nurse tucked him in, making him quite comfortable. The minute he was left alone, he propped himself up on one elbow, painfully and laboriously, to look out the window.

It faced a blank wall.

✔ Application:

When you watch TV or go to the movies, do you ever get the feeling that everybody in the world is experiencing a lot more of life than you are? That they are having all the fun, doing all the exciting things, winning all the prizes, getting all the good stuff? That's exactly what the media wants you to feel like. That's what keeps you coming back for more.

When we live our lives vicariously through the media, which is many people's window on the world, we begin to feel as Mr. Thayer did—resentful and envious. We become dangerously self-centered. We begin to feel deprived of what should rightfully be ours, and we become more and more dissatisfied with life.

More often than not, we're taken in by the images of a reality that doesn't exist—images the media projects on a blank wall. These images represent a world that doesn't exist. When we try to live like the images that we see or try to obtain all the stuff that the commercials tell us to buy, we end up terribly disappointed. Why? Because it's nothing more than an illusion flickering on a blank wall.

Jesus came to set us free from illusion. He came so that we could live life to its fullest, as it really is. (See John 10:10.) He doesn't tease us with empty promises. Instead He came to tell us the truth about ourselves, the truth about the world we live in, and the truth about God. "I am the way and the truth and the life . . . " (John 14:6).

Wrong Way Riegels

On New Year's Day, 1929, Georgia Tech played UCLA in the Rose Bowl. In that game a UCLA player named Roy Riegels recovered a fumble, but somehow got confused and started running in the wrong direction down the field. He ran sixty-five yards before one of his teammates, Benny Lom, tackled him just in front of the goal line—otherwise Riegels could have scored a safety for the opposing team. UCLA was unable to move the ball from that point in the game. Georgia Tech blocked the punt and scored a safety on the play.

Since that strange play happened in the first half, everyone watching the game was asking the same question: "What will Coach Nibbs Price do with Roy Riegels in the second half?" The players filed off the field, went into the dressing room, and sat down on the benches and the floor—all except Riegels. He put his blanket around his shoulders, sat down in a corner, put his face in his hands, and cried like a baby.

A coach usually has a great deal to say to his team during halftime, but that day, Coach Price was quiet. No doubt he was trying to decide what to do

with Riegels. Then the timekeeper came in and announced that there were only three minutes till play time. Price looked at the team and said simply, "Men, the same team that played the first half will start the second."

The players got up and started out—all but Riegels. He didn't budge. The coach looked back and called to him again; still he didn't move. Coach

Price went over to where Riegels sat and said, "Roy, didn't you hear me? The same team that played the first half will start the second." Then Roy Riegels looked up and Price saw that his cheeks were wet with a strong man's tears.

"Coach," he said, "I can't do it to save my life. I've ruined you. I've ruined the University of California. I've ruined myself. I couldn't face that crowd in the stadium to save my life."

Then Coach Price put his hand on Riegels' shoulder and said, "Roy, get up and go on back. The game is only half over." And Roy Riegels went back, and those Georgia Tech players will tell you they have never seen a man play football as Roy Riegels did in that second half.

(From "A Little Phrase for Losers" by Haddon Robinson in *Christianity Today*, October 26, 1992.)

☑ Application:

The grace of God is like Roy's coach. At times we feel as if we've messed up so badly that we want to give up and throw in the towel. God doesn't give up on us, though. He says, "Get up and get on out there. The game isn't over yet." The Gospel of the grace of God is the Gospel of the second chance, and the third chance, and the hundredth chance. We fumble the ball continually, but God never tosses us out of the game. He just keeps cheering us on.

You, Too, Can Be Beautiful

    Actress Michelle Pfeiffer appeared on the cover of a magazine with the caption "What Michele Pfeiffer Needs Is . . . Absolutely Nothing!"

    It was later discovered by a reporter, however, that Michelle Pfeiffer did need something after all. She needed over $1500 worth of touch-up work on that cover photo. From the touch-up artist's bill, here is a partial list of things that were done to make Michelle Pfeiffer look beautiful:

    Clean up complexion, soften eye lines, soften smile line, add color to lips, trim chin, remove neck lines, soften line under earlobe, add highlights to earrings, add blush to cheek, clean up neckline, remove stray hair, remove hair strands on dress, adjust color and add hair on top of head, add dress on side to create better line, add forehead, add dress on shoulder, soften neck muscle a bit, clean up and smooth dress folds under arm, and create one seam on image on right side.

Total price: $1,525.00

✓ Application:

Anybody can be beautiful with a $1500 touch-up job! We need to be careful that we don't compare ourselves unfavorably with media stars and people who appear to be perfect and to have it all together. Those people are just like you and me—they have a deep longing inside for love and meaning. Many of them believe that they can find love and meaning by being famous or glamorous. Don't believe the lie. "Man looks at the outward appearance, but the Lord looks at the heart" (I Sam. 16:7b).

WE WANT YOUR HOT ILLUSTRATION!

If you have an effective illustration that you have used in youth talks and are willing to share it with others, send it to Youth Specialties and we'll publish it in *Hot Illustrations for Youth Talks, Volume Two!*

Illustrations like those in this book are welcome, but we are also interested in quotes, jokes, object lessons, and other creative ways to communicate with kids. Turn your illustrations into cash by sending them to:

Hot Illustrations
Youth Specialties
1224 Greenfield Drive
El Cajon, CA 92021

INDEX TO TOPICS